FOLLOWING
THE WAY

BRUCE E. SCHEIN

FOLLOWING THE WAY

THE SETTING OF JOHN'S GOSPEL

Augsburg Publishing House
Minneapolis, Minnesota

In memory of
Grandma Busch
who first showed me
the love of the study of the Way.

FOLLOWING THE WAY
1980 First American Edition
Augsburg Publishing House
Copyright © 1980 Sadan Publishing House
Library of Congress Catalog Card No. 79-54121
International Standard Book No. 0-8066-1758-6

Scripture quotations are from the Revised Standard Version of the Bible, copyright 1946, 1952 and 1971 by the Division of Christian Education of the National Council of Churches. Quotations from John other than chapter 12 are the author's translation. Quotations from the Apocrypha and Deuteronomical books on p. 95, 40, 100 are from R.H. Charles, *The Apocrypha and Pseudepigrapha of the Old Testament in English,* Vol. II, Pseudepigrapha, Oxford, Clarendon Press, 1913. Quotation on p. 119 is from H. Danby, *The Mishnah,* Oxford University Press, 1938, reprint 1972.

PHOTOGRAPHY: AVRAHAM HAY

ILLUSTRATIONS
Drawings: M. Gabrieli (29, 59, 60–61, 77, 89, 141, 165, 173);
H. Ron (175, 178, 185, 207, 208).
Maps: (21, 30, 51, 71, 83, 99, 115, 142, 149, 192, 204, 210, 213).
Copyright © Sadan 1980.
Design: Yishai Afek

ACKNOWLEDGMENTS
The publishers wish to thank the following for permission to reproduce illustrations (numbers in brackets refer to pages in this book): The Israel Exploration Society, Jerusalem, *The Madaba Map,* Michael Avi-Yonah, 1953 (188, 212); *Jerusalem Revealed,* 1975, reconstruction by B. Lalor (123, 199); The Holyland Hotel, "The Jerusalem Model" by Michael Avi-Yonah; Edward Hill (176). The satellite background for all the maps in this book printed by permission of Survey of Israel.

CONTENTS

A fragment
including a passage
from the Gospel
according to Saint
John chapter 18.
This fragment of
papyrus goes back
to about 130 A.D.

Preface

*That which was from the beginning,
which we have heard, which we have seen
with our eyes, which we have looked upon
and touched with our hands, concerning
the word of life — the life was made
manifest, and we saw it, and testify to it,
and proclaim to you the eternal life which
was with the Father and was made
manifest to us — that which we have seen
and heard we proclaim also to you, so
that you may have fellowship with us;
and our fellowship is with the Father and
with His Son Jesus Christ. And we are
writing this that your joy may be
complete.*

1 John 1:1—4

How amazing that modern study of the Gospel according to Saint John could so easily either ignore this opening statement of the First Letter of John, or twist its straightforward expression. John has probably been the most neglected Gospel in terms of the *touchable and seeable background* of the first century. The great geographies of the New Testament like Dalman's classic *Orte und Wege Jesu (The Places and Ways of Jesus)* usually employ the first three Gospels, the Synoptics, as their frame. John often seems "stuck in" to describe important events not mentioned by the other Evangelists. In other fields of New Testament studies, such blending of Gospels is never tolerated, for it loses the specific point of view of each Evangelist. Articles such as W. F. Albright's "Recent Discoveries in Palestine and the Gospel of St. John" (in *The Background of the New Testament and its Eschatology*), or a chapter devoted to John in works like W. D. Davies' *The Gospel and the Land,* which deal with the geography of John's Gospel are relatively few. This is remarkable, for John constantly keeps the reader informed with precise geographical data. This

7

neglect of Johannine geography, however, is not solely of recent vintage. We still seem to labor under Clement of Alexandria's description of John as the *Spiritual Gospel*. This has resulted in a tendency to symbolize, spiritualize, or simply ignore all the down-to-earth "facts" in the Gospel so that, free of its earth-binding luggage, it might soar.

This book began 14 years ago when I first lived in the geographic setting of John's Gospel. My experience with the region during the ensuing years has made shallow treatment of its geography impossible. The neglect of the environment of John disturbs me, particularly since many who brush it aside often seem culturally and physically ingrained in their western culture and setting. Having received the opportunity for postdoctoral study and teaching of the historical geography of the Holy Land in Jerusalem during this decade, my uneasiness has led to the determination to help fill a somewhat empty portion of Johannine studies. To be sure, this vacuum is already being reduced by some recent commentaries such as the excellent work in English by R. E. Brown, or that in French by M. E. Boismard. J. A. T. Robinson's recent suggestions for an early date for John's Gospel and his concern that its author be considered an eyewitness, indicate that it is indeed time to reevaluate the physical aspects of the Gospel. This book should help pastors and laypeople in that process of reevaluation.

The search for a suitable format has not been easy. The decision to describe the setting as if one is present in first-century Palestine was made because the Gospel never simply recounts place names any more than it merely clicks off Old Testament proof texts. Detail is faithfully employed to spark deeper and broader thoughts. This indicates that John expects the reader to have some familiarity with the setting of Jesus' ministry, or be associated with people who still vividly recall it. This would indicate that John may well be one of the earliest Gospels.

This corner of the globe is often referred to as the "Holy Land" because every inch of it seems literally covered with layers of the experiences of God's People. The interaction of the land and events would be felt by the first-century disciples much the same as by my school boys on a hike. To enter into this "feeling" *with and for the land* with eyes, ears, hands, and hearts is important for a complete understanding of the Johannine setting. After all, that is precisely what the First Letter of John indicates.

The problems involved in reconstructing that setting are considerable. Much of the reconstruction depends not on other first-century descriptions of the land (which are embarrassingly few), but rather on archaeological study and one's actual experience of the ancient ways. The resulting picture must constantly be changed as fresh discoveries are made. An effort, however, must be made to reconstruct a whole picture from the available fragments, rather than leaving a mere hodgepodge of interesting finds. Certainly this is one of the tasks of the geographer of the New Testament.

In this method of presentation, the exegesis and the setting are combined. These two are not separate, for the salient feature of the settings (which have been carefully selected by the author of the Gospel, John 20:30-31) is their fundamental importance for the message. John's genius, as his use of the Old Testament and legends also demonstrates, is to so master his material and make it so much a part of himself, that his exegesis does not obtrude, but blends perfectly with the "facts." John begins with the concrete, which is entirely geographical, and extracts from these hard facts the inner meaning and experience they contain. This is exactly the method of Jesus' teaching in the Gospel. Observations on earthly objects or events reveal the meaning of His heavenly message.

So that the text of John may be followed as the reconstruction unfolds, references are given in upper case letters in the margin. Unless indicated the quotations from John are my translations. All other quotes follow the Revised Standard Version of the Bible. The references in *italics* are to other Biblical passages (including the Apocrypha), as well as cross references to John. These italicized references also include other important ancient writings. *The Mishnah* which records the opinions of Rabbis during the first centuries A.D. is an important source for the ritual of the feasts observed in Jesus' day. This is available in several English translations. *Enoch, The Ascension of Isaiah, Testament of the Twelve Patriarchs,* and *2 Baruch* will be found in English in R. H. Charles' *Pseudepigrapha of the Old Testament.* These writings come from the Roman period, but are not included in the Bible or Apocrypha. Any attempt to understand the geography of the Gospel of John must also take into account the legends that made the land and Scripture live for the People of God then, even as they do to this day. Often people are more familiar with the legends that grow around the Biblical characters, than with the actual Biblical stories themselves. John's original audience (and Jesus' for that matter) would have known these popular tales and understood the passing, but important, references to them. They are called *Midrashim.* Fortunately a great number of these are available in English in the invaluable *Midrash Rabbah* (Soncino Press, ed. M. Simon). *Midrashim* will also be noted in the margin. Every geographer of the New Testament is greatly indebted to Josephus who knew Palestine before the Romans destroyed Jerusalem in A.D. 70. He is our only detailed source for much of the setting of first-century Palestine and (in spite of a tendency to exaggerate when recounting events) is accurate in most geographical details. His writings are available in English translation in the Loeb Classical Library. The *Jewish War* which is most often referred to in the margin is available in several paperback editions. These background references are essential for a full understanding of a particular setting or event.

Appendices have been provided to show how some locations were chosen or reconstructed. There is also a selected bibliography to help initiate further study. The proper spelling of names is always a problem when dealing with the geography of the Holy Land. We will follow the RSV for all Biblical names and Avi-Yonah's *Gazetteer of Roman Palestine* for all others.

Understanding the geography of John's Gospel demands more than a study of place references. One needs a feel for the entire land during the period of Jesus' ministry. This is the important and larger backdrop which gives added meaning to individually highlighted sites and ways. Flora, fauna, customs, and manners form essential parts of that background. First-century Palestine is not the same as either the Old Testament, or the modern world. Simply, this means that sites, customs, and geological formations must be described as much as possible in their first-century form. Archaeology has revealed that certain first-century assumptions concerning *where* or even *how* earlier events took place are false. We cannot use such archaeological correctives in a reconstruction. We must see first-century Palestine as its people knew it.

A word about "ways." When reading the Bible, we rush over seemingly simple statements like: "The Judeans sent priests and Levites (from Jerusalem) to ask him (John the Baptist in Bethany of Peraea) 'Who are you?'" (John 1:19). We need to slow down our reading. There is so much in that three-second statement to think about! Anyone who has spent hours walking on the way to Jericho knows this. The world during a twelve-hour hike moves by slowly. Actually, this slow-paced time is hardly enough even to begin to comprehend the historical and natural reminders that pack the way from familiar place names to sudden dramatic shifts in landscape. Every way has its distinctive personality. This intertwining of places, events, and nature through the sweep of the history of God's People is important to John. This becomes clear in the very first chapter, as the setting of the Baptist's ministry at the end of the Jerusalem-Jericho way both raises and destroys expectations. This is not surprising, but rather is expected from someone who has seen and touched this land.

The maps which appear throughout the book are actually satellite pictures. Only the ways and places dealt with in the chapter itself are given in the map. This will facilitate easy reference. The exact route followed by Jesus is not given in the Gospel, for it is assumed that the reader knows it. Fortunately, many ancient roads are still known and others can be fairly well determined. It is possible that Jesus made detours or used odd routes. However, we have kept to the normal ways between first century villages and cities.

There are probably as many theories about the authorship and state of the "original" Fourth Gospel and its sources as there are New Testament scholars. It is not our purpose to deal with that issue, although it is hoped this study may stimulate reconsiderations when new theories are proposed. We have found that geographical grounds provide a shaky foundation for building any theory of rearrangement of the text or positing of many editors. We will follow the order of chapters as they appear in the Bible. It is important, no matter what theories of editing are proposed, that the Gospel be understood in its canonical form as used in the life of the Church.

It has been a great pleasure to work with Avraham Hay on photography and Mordechai Gabrieli on the illustrations. The assistance of Edward Peterson, Diana Schein, and my mother in preparing the final manuscript has been invaluable. The research for this work was made possible by the German Evangelical Archaeological Institute in Jerusalem where I was privileged to serve as assistant director under Ute Lux. The members of my Lutheran Church in America Holy Land Seminars (teachers of the Bible from around the world) have provided many fresh insights into the text from their varied cultural viewpoints and methods of interpretation.

The persons to whom I am most indebted are my students from St. Olaf College of Northfield, Minnesota. For the past five years, during their semester abroad, they have enthusiastically put on their hiking boots and walked all the ways of the Fourth Gospel — and a couple of extra miles. They have struggled along with me, sweating, freezing, meditating, joking, singing, and, yes, sometimes even crying from the pain, sorrow — and joy of it all! They are students who would have made that simple, loving teacher to whose memory this book is dedicated, very proud.

Bruce E. Schein
Redeemer Church
Jerusalem, Old City
The Feast of Saint John
1979

chapter one

The Beginning

In the beginning, John's Gospel gives the feeling of the breaking forth of a New Creation. This impression is created, not only by the echoing of the first chapter of Genesis in the opening poem of the Gospel, but also by the choice of the lower part of the Jordan Valley for the opening scene. The steep, stark hills on either side of that desert valley, along with the harsh, austere landscape, the thin life-giving green line of the winding Jordan River as it cuts through white chalk mounds in the valley's center, the pungent odor of the salty sea — even the heavy air of the region evokes the feeling of the process of creation. *JOHN 1:1*

Often, just before dawn or in the late afternoon, there is a lighting effect in the skies that further reminds one of the story of creation. It is a primordial illumination that emanates from the Creator, for its source seems to be beyond sun or moon. Such was the First Day of Creation, and *God saw that it was good.* *Gen. 1:1-5* *Gen. 1*

Throughout the day, the blue upper sky divides itself from the lower haze hanging directly above the valley. When viewed from the heights of the valley's sides, it appears as if there is an ocean of air above the world divided from a sea of air below. The firmament above is divided from the firmament below. So was the Second Day of Creation, and *God saw that it was good.* *Gen. 1:6-8*

More than any other terrain, the desert brings our thoughts back to the basics of life and to the understanding that there is a Force greater than ourselves and the world about us. In the desert we find ourselves utterly dependent upon this Force, for it is the source of lifegiving water and protective shade. In a land of arid rock and dirt, we are awed by the miracle of the green oasis brought forth by a spring which seems to come from nothing.

In the Jordan Valley one sees signs of the original division of dry land and water. Occasionally, the imprint of a seashell can be found on a loose piece of limestone, a reminder that 130 million years ago a sea covered the valley and the land to the west. In the ancient sea bed, deep deposits of limestone from shells and other marine life accumulated, layer by layer, building a thickness in certain places of 2,000 feet. A weak line in the earth's surface gave way to this enormous load of limestone, and a deep depression appeared in the area where the valley floor would one day lie. Some 55 million years ago, a huge ripple on the earth's surface accelerated this sinking process as it forced up the land on its sides. Thus the high hills on either side of the valley gradually rose and separated themselves from the sea.

At first, an island of dry land appeared between the Great Sea and the inland lake which filled the deep depression. Then the lake began to drain, leaving chalky hillocks at its bottom which remind the traveler that water once filled the valley. Ten million years ago, as the floor of the valley continued to sink, there was a final, terrible wrenching motion when the hills on the east side of the valley

Left:
A lighting effect just before dawn, outlines the austere desert land in the lower part of the Jordan Valley.

13

Above:
A contrast to the Dead Sea and the barren hills, is the greenery of the oases on both sides of the Jordan.

Left:
The raven is one of the few wild birds that is strong enough to tolerate the harsh life of the desert.

Upper left:
The imprint of the seashell on a loose piece of limestone, a reminder that 130 million years ago a sea covered the Jordan Valley and the land to the west.

Lower left:
The first evidence of man's social awareness—the remains of the towers and wall of Jericho, believed to be the oldest city in the world, built about 10,000 years ago.

were shoved 25 miles to the north, leaving the deepest gash in the earth's crust. The lake now was reduced to the small Sea of Galilee which collected the water drained from the resulting hills and mountains. The Jordan River was created to carry the lake's overflow through the lower Jordan Valley merely to come to a dead end in a salt sea in which no life can exist. This Dead Sea, formed only 10,000 years ago, indicates how recent is the creation of this area.

Gen. 1:9-13

What a contrast to the Dead Sea and the surrounding barren hills is the greenery of the plains on either side of the Jordan! From the desert floor of the valley, oases spring up with their brilliantly colored flowers and stately palms. In March, the month our Gospel begins, there is a further sign of life appearing on the dry land. The valley's sides are covered by a fuzzy green velvet of winter grass studded with gemlike flowers in light pinks, blues, and yellows. This fragile life seems to spring from the rocks themselves — truly life begotten from nothing. Such was the Third Day of Creation, and *God saw that it was good.*

Gen. 1:14-19

Many have noted that the heavenly hosts somehow appear to be closer to earth as they shine above the valley. Perhaps it is the desert's starkness or the heights of the valley's sides that creates such an impression. Sometimes at midnight, one or two brilliant stars seem near enough to touch. At noon, the closeness of the sun is felt even more as its rays beat unrelentingly on one's head. From time to time there is a most remarkable sight. In midmorning the moon can be seen clearly on the other side of the heavens. This nearness of sun, moon, and stars gives one a feeling of their part in the total creation. They do not stand apart as the rulers and creators of the earth, which is the belief of the pagans. They are not first in the order of Creation but Fourth, and *their Maker saw that they were good.*

Gen. 1:20-23

The harsh life of the desert by the Dead Sea and west of the mouth of the Jordan can be tolerated only by strong birds such as the raven. As this large bird soars with huge black wings spread against the heat looking for scraps of nourishment from the castoffs of creation, one also is reminded of life at its most basic. His strident cry is far from the gentle and refined lyric melody of the delicately-colored birds which cling to the luxurious oases. He cries for fundamental necessities. It is the cry of independence of one who did not need to return to the safety of the ark as the earth lay flooded by water, and dry land had not yet appeared. What a contrast the raven is to the soft and delicate dove that flutters by the springs in the valley floor or nests in the rocky sides of the openings into the Jordan Valley. The dove never ventures far, but clings to the shelter of the shaded cleft and close to the water and plants of the desert's life-filled sanctuaries. This is a creature well-suited to carry in its beak greenery such as an olive branch, proclaiming life in a land of death. Raven and dove together mark well the Fifth Day as their primal cry and peaceful cooing mingle to proclaim that *God's Creation is good.*

Right:
A bird's eye view
of the River
Jordan.

Perhaps what is most impressive in the area where our Gospel begins is not the natural beauty set forth in such sharp, elemental contrasts. Rather it is a huge pile of dirt which dominates the plain to the west of the Jordan River. A forceful, life-giving spring pours forth from its base to sustain the plants whose fragrance gives the area its name, Jericho, *Sweet Smelling*. In the center of this mound stand a tower and city wall built about 10,000 years ago. These are the remains

16

of the oldest city in the world. Here was one of the first places our ancestors learned the meaning of society and what it is to share and cooperate in order to tend well the beautiful paradisaical garden surrounding them. *God saw that it was good* that these people should be the caretakers of His Creation. Such was the Sixth Day.

Gen. 1:24-31

On the Seventh Day, the Sabbath, *having completed the Good Creation, God rested.*

Gen. 2:1-3

Strabo, a Roman geographer living in the first century A.D., compares the end of the Jordan Valley to a theater. As one looks across the Jordan River from the hills which rise behind Jericho, the Plains of Moab appear as a gigantic stage, with the hills of the east side of the Jordan Valley forming the tiers of seats arranged in a huge semicircle around it. The pagan Strabo never appreciated how doubly accurate was his description. The Plains of Moab became the great stage for the awaited drama of salvation for God's People.

Geography 16.2,41

As John's Gospel begins on a March morning in A.D. 28, the eyes of the People of God are focused on this stage where the great and final act of God's redemptive work is awaited. Salvation is needed because human actions in history from Adam until this moment constitute a tragedy. People continually turn from their responsibility as caretakers of the good creation to the worship of the creation itself and their own power. To be sure, there were hopeful moments in the drama. Many of these moments were played out on the stage of the Plains of Moab. At Shittim, Moses had proclaimed a new beginning for the People waiting to cross the Jordan and enter the land of milk and honey. After making his proclamation, he climbed to the top seats at the south of the stage, Mount Nebo, as if to wait for the unfolding of the ensuing drama. Generation after generation would look to Mount Nebo as they recalled God's promise that another prophet like Moses would arise to *lead the way.*

Deut. 34:1-12

Deut. 18:18

From Shittim Joshua had *led forth the way* across the Plains of Moab, over the Jordan River, and into the Promised Land. A second entry is now awaited, for the first had ended in tragedy. The victories of the conquering Joshua were short-lived as much infighting broke out among the People. Their weakness resulted first in the loss of the northern tribes, united as Israel, and finally, some six centuries after the entry of Joshua, in the loss of Judah. The defeated leaders of Judah were led to the east as captives of a great pagan nation.

Joshua 1-4

The defeat of Judah in turn fired new hopes. A grand procession is expected to pass again through the center of our stage as the People return in final victory with an anointed one leading them. This new Joshua (or Jesus in Greek) would end the terrible occupation and oppression which followed the destruction of Israel and Judah. This new leader would be what the name Joshua-Jesus means, — *Salvation.* The present subjugation to the western imperialistic power, Rome, is felt everywhere. In fact, not far from the site of Shittim where the followers of Joshua had gathered, a Roman city named after Livias, the wife of Augustus Caesar, has been established. An end to this pagan domination is eagerly awaited. This will take place when a final savior, a new Joshua-Jesus, arises to *lead the way.*

At center stage, not far from the Jordan River is a small village called Bethany. This well-watered area holds the greatest promise of a repeat

Bethany

18

performance. A chariot of fire had once descended here to transport the prophet *2 Kings 2:1-12* Elijah to heaven. This mortal who never tasted death will be the one to usher in the great day of a new creation. He will *lead the way* before the anointed one in the great victory parade to Jerusalem on that final day of conquest. As a new *Malachi 4:5* day breaks over the Plains of Moab on a March morning, the sun illuminates the stage for the beginning of that long-awaited drama of a new creation.

In the beginning was the Word
and the Word was with God,
and God was the Word.
He was in the beginning with God.
Everything came into being through Him
and apart from Him, nothing came into being.
In Him was Life
and the Life was the Light of humanity.
The Light shines in the darkness,
and the darkness could not grasp It...

The Light coming into the world was
the true Light which enlightens everyone.
He was in the world
and the world came into being through Him,
yet, the world did not know Him.
He came to His own
and His own people did not receive Him.
But whoever received Him,
whoever believed in His name,
He gave to them the authority to be Children of God,
who were begotten not from blood,
nor from the desire of the flesh,
nor from the desire of men, but from God.
And the Word became flesh and tabernacled among us.
We have seen His glory,
glory as the Only-begotten of the Father,
full of favor and truth....

With the result that from His completeness
we receive favor upon favor.
The law was given through Moses;
favor and truth came through Jesus, the Anointed One.
No one has ever seen God, the only-begotten Son,
Who is in the bosom of the Father,
this One *leads the way.*

John 1:1 f

JOHN 1:1-5, 9-14, 16-18

A great river issuing from under the altar rock in Jerusalem will overflow the banks of the Kidron Valley.

JOHN 1:19

2 Sam. 15:13-16:14

2 Kings 25:1-7

At dawn on this first day of the new creation, priests together with Levites, the other order of officiants in the Temple, climb the Mount of Olives. So begins the well-worn 18-mile way to Jericho. This will lead them to their destination, Bethany on the other side of the Jordan River. This ancient pathway itself underscores the urgency of their mission. This is to question a certain John about the purpose of his ministry of baptism. The great king David once "went forth" over the Kidron Valley and up the Mount of Olives in defeat and humiliation as his own son, Absalom, sought to wrest the kingdom from him. He climbed this way with his head covered and his feet bare, weeping as he went. The last king of Judah also was forced to escape along this way. After being chased by the Babylonians, he was captured at Jericho. With eyes gouged out, he was led from there over the Jordan and to the east at the head of the rest of the exiles. This way of defeat in turn sparked a hope that one day it would become the victory route of a new David, an anointed one who would be the great and final king of the Judeans.

As the traveler turns at the top of the Mount of Olives to view the city for the last time before beginning the descent to Jericho, he is conscious of the continued oppression of God's People by the Roman military machine. Attention is drawn from the Temple to the Antonia, the huge barracks and headquarters of the Roman soldiers. This mammoth shrine to human power dwarfs the sanctuary to the south of it. On the western side of the city, its highest and most strategic area, the three massive towers in the curve of the city wall are bathed in the floodlight of the rising sun, making these ominous sentinels of Roman domination even more threatening. The beautiful palace complex of Caesar's representative in Jerusalem, the procurator, lies to the south under their protection. The dramatic beauty of its clean, white limestone buildings extends along three-quarters of the skyline of Jerusalem and further distracts from the Temple.

20

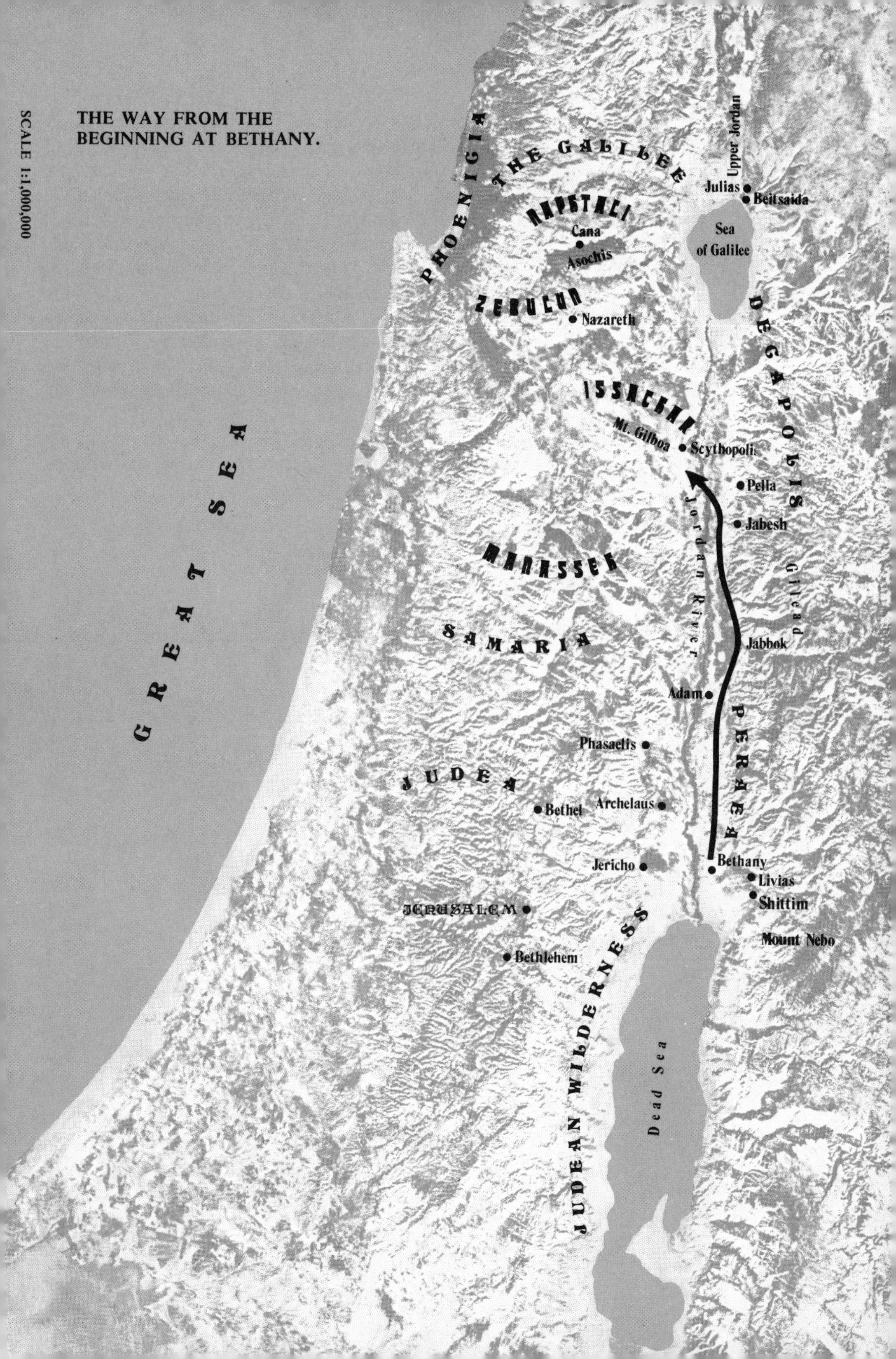

THE WAY FROM THE BEGINNING AT BETHANY.

SCALE 1:1,000,000

Thoughts turn to the prophet's promise of liberation from such pagan oppression when the Mount of Olives will split open for the King of Kings to enter in final victory over the forces of evil. As the long descent on the other side of the Mount of Olives is begun, further hopes of that victorious entry of the Anointed One are aroused. Isaiah promised that the rugged desert of Judea stretched out before the traveler will become a gigantic ramp as the valleys are lifted up and the hills made low. This is to be the great entryway of the Lord.

The Levites and priests climb yet another small but tiring rise just past the halfway point of the still-to-be-smoothed highway that drops off rapidly to Jericho. Here the landscape itself raises expectations. Even after the winter rains, the little green that does manage to appear along this way is often obscured by the brown hills of the Judean desert. Here is the domain of dust and thorns, mute reminders of a paradise lost.

Again it is the hopeless which nurtures hope! The prophets describe how a new paradise will be created here from whence people never again will be driven

Zech. 14:3-5

Is. 40:3-5

Gen. 3:17-19

Ezek. 47:1-12

out. The transformation will come when a great river issuing from under the altar rock in Jerusalem will overflow the banks of the Kidron Valley. These desert hills will not only be carpeted in thick grass and lined with groves of fruit-bearing trees. They will also be decked with cascading grapevines and drip with sweet wine! This vision is sharpened as Jericho's green palm groves come into the background. Such greenery produced on the desert floor of the valley by a few powerful springs is like that which will one day enliven and shade the way from Jerusalem. The excitement born of that hope multiplies as the area of Bethany across the Jordan comes into view. Perhaps in Bethany an Elijah might be found ready to lead an anointed one up the ramp through the vineyards of a regained paradise to reign in a liberated Jerusalem. The Baptist's choice of the stage for his ministry swells these hopes.

When the priests and Levites arrive at Bethany and make their query, the answer is not only disappointing, it is completely bewildering. John denies any connection with the great figures of hope to which this area points. He is not

Zech. 14:8

Amos 9:13-14

Streched out before the traveler are the rugged desert hills of Judea.

another Joshua from Shittim, or the anointed one from the East about to cross over the Jordan for the final entry into the Promised Land. He is not a prophet like Moses come down from Nebo to proclaim a new world. Most shattering, John is not even the returned prophet Elijah whose place of departure he chose for his ministry. Who then is he? As the barren hills across the Jordan press down on the oases-filled desert of the valley floor, the answer rings out. He is the
voice in the desert crying: "Make straight the way of the Lord." As the questioners look around at the water flowing near Bethany and note the green
trees lining the nearby Jordan where he has baptized so many, they are naturally led to the next question: "Why then are you baptizing?" The answer is no less bewildering than his first claim. He is preparing for One Who is coming Whose
dirty sandal he is not worthy to loosen.

On the day after this shattering of all expectations, the second day, John
begins to point to that One. He describes Him as the Lamb. During these March days lambs are much in evidence as they are being fattened on the fresh winter grass. The firstborn of these will soon be slaughtered at the Passover festival. John points at this time of preparation for Passover to a Jesus of Nazareth, designating Him as the Lamb Who takes away the sin of the world. John is certain of His identity, for he has seen the Spirit descend upon Him like a dove. People consider this representation of the Spirit a perfect creature because its body is thought to contain no bile. The dove lives near the springs in the desert such as those around Bethany. Its presence assures travelers of the presence of the source of life.

On the third day the designation of the Lamb is made again. This time two
disciples of John respond and follow Him. These first disciples of Jesus are gathered in the semi-pagan region across the Jordan, Peraea, which is outside of Judea and the Promised Land. Thoughts of Joshua and the gathering of the People for the entry into the land begin to arouse expectations. After all, He Whom Greek-speaking people call Jesus is called *Joshua* in Hebrew. Could this be the beginning of a force led by a new Joshua-Jesus?

The first followers, Andrew and John, stay with Him on the fourth day.
Soon more follow. Andrew's brother joins, receiving a new name, a new personality at this beginning. Cephas is to be his name, or Peter in its Greek form which is translated *Rock*. The home of these brothers, Bethsaida, is east of the upper Jordan River in the pagan-dominated territory of Philip the Tetrarch. Bethsaida, *Place of Fishing,* is actually the port for one of the major cities in Philip's territory, Julias. Like Livias near Bethany, this city's name also serves to remind one of Rome's dominating presence.

On the fifth day, as this small group starts out for the Galilee, possibly
having completed a business trip to Jerusalem, another citizen of Bethsaida, Philip, is called to follow Jesus. His name reflects well the influences at work in Bethsaida. Philip was also the name of the father of Alexander the Great who brought Hellenic paganism to the east in the first place. This bearer of a pagan name immediately goes to one who has a most suitable name for a follower of the
true God, Nathanael, *Gift of God*. Nathanael's hometown, Cana, is part of the former northern tribal alliance, Israel, located in the largest of the northern tribes, Naphtali. The pride of one who lives beside the richest valley in the hills of the

lower Galilee, the Asochis Plain, is felt in his sarcastic response to Philip. He wonders whether any good can come out of that tiny, half-forgotten village of Nazareth which is tucked up in the hills of the former tribe of Zebulun, a tribe evidently so weak that it could not take its rightful place in Phoenicia by the Great Sea. Jesus greets this skeptic quite appropriately, for truly he is an Israelite and straightforward at that. How does Jesus know him? He claims to have seen Nathanael under a fig tree before Philip called him. How fitting is his resting place, for the fig tree is a sign of hope. Only the fig and the grape have leaves broad enough to offer the weary cool shade during the beating heat of the day. It is under the fig tree that one will sit at peace with his neighbors in the days of the new paradise. Jesus' words kindle Nathanael's hopes and suddenly he sees before him the Bringer of that new creation. Here is the King of Israel!

Gen. 49:13

Micah 4:4

Zech. 3:10

His acclamation is not unequivocally accepted. As the newly-formed band of disciples leaves Bethany of Peraea and moves north toward the Galilee along the east side of the valley, Jesus directs their gaze across the Jordan River to the way leading up to Bethel. He points to the high ridge where Jacob-Israel dreamed of heaven and earth united. In that vision, so the text may be understood, it is not the ladder to which the pronoun refers as that upon which the angels ascended and descended. Rather it is Jacob himself. Both *ladder* and *Jacob* are expressed by the pronoun *he* in the Hebrew text of Genesis. It is possible to understand Jacob as the connecting link between heaven and earth as the angels ascend and descend upon *him*. Jesus informs Nathanael that he will see more than a King of Israel. He will view the angels ascending and descending upon Him Who is the link between heaven and earth!

Gen. 28:10-17

The high ridge where Jacob-Israel dreamed of heaven.

25

This fifth day is spent walking through the Jordan Valley. It is an easy walk with no hills to climb. In March it can be pleasantly warm except, of course, for the heat of midday. The flat valley and unvaried landscape lend themselves to reflection and conversation in order to pass the time. As they walk the disciples begin to learn from their new Rabbi. The way between Bethany and the Jabbok River leads through dry land with no springs. Across the Jordan the huge palm plantations of the northern half of the Jericho Plain between the cities of Archelaus and Phasaelis present a strong contrast. Here is the fording place of Adam, where once the waters were blocked so that Joshua could enter the Promised Land on a dry riverbed. There is no desire to cross. Rather, one is relieved to be on the other side. The hills of Samaria mark the end of Judea, bringing the other side of the Jordan, north of Adam, into Samaritan territory. The Samaritan hills are a painful reminder of the division of the People of God through the centuries. Samaritans, after all, are the remnant of Israel which was

JOHN 2:1

Josh. 3:15-17

26

once united with Judah by David and Solomon. An anointed one is awaited who will bring reconciliation to the People of God, removing the hatred between north and south, Judean and Samaritan. Perhaps if again united, they could cast out the Romans whose fortresses dominate Samaria as well as Judea. *Is. 11:13*

Soon the Jabbok River is reached. This symbolizes just such a reconciliation between brothers. Here the returning Jacob met Esau, his estranged brother, and received his forgiveness. It was here that Jacob's name was changed as Simon's had been changed yesterday. Jacob crossed the Jordan as *Israel* whose name the north had proudly kept for its territory. To be sure, there also had been tragedy in the area of the Jabbok and north of it in the hills of Gilead. Here the escaping David sent his forces against his son Absalom. In the resulting battle, Absalom was killed. That bitter victory meant that David could again unite the country under Jerusalem's control. Yet, as the disciples move further north along the valley, the hills of Gilead rising on their right side symbolize more the healing that might one day come to Samaria which faces them on the west. *Gen. 32:3-33:18* *2 Sam. 18:1-20:22*

In these hills fine medicinal herbs are found which were used by many nations in earlier times. Is there no balm in Gilead to heal the divisions among the People of God? Could this Jesus Whom the disciples follow to the Galilee be the physician for the People of God? Such might be the thoughts of the Judea-oriented disciples as they pause to rest for the night somewhere near the Jabesh River which flows from the hills of Gilead. At Jabesh, after all, there has been a people who understood the importance of being united against the pagan forces. They had called the first king, Saul, to rescue them from such a threat. They repaid Saul's help in saving them by bringing his body here following his death at the hands of the Philistines. That threat of paganism still is not removed, for the disciples are in the area now called the Decapolis, *Ten Cities,* which prides itself in upholding Greek culture and religion in the East. *Jer. 8:22* *1 Sam. 11:1-10* *1 Sam. 31:11-13*

At the beginning of the sixth day, Joshua-Jesus and his followers finally cross the Jordan and enter the Promised Land. How different is this crossing from that of the first Joshua! There is no drying up of the waters of the Jordan. The fording place is easy. There is no need for a ramp to lead into the center of the country. The gently rising, broad Valley of Jezreel welcomes the disciples. Nor is there any need for a water-swollen Kidron to make barren, desert-topped hills green. The rich, black volcanic soil, watered by abundant springs and rivulets pouring from the green hills of Gilboa and collected by the Valley of Jezreel, produces a lushness in March that is a paradise for the senses. Fields of grain are green, thick, and high. Pools are formed here and there in which birds can bathe. The hills of Gilboa behind the entry plain and valley dazzle the viewer with a variety of spring flowers spread out like a huge patchwork quilt of reds, blues, yellows, and whites. Fat sheep in large flocks, and herds of cattle, a rare sight in the south, feast on the luxury about them. This area, part of the former tribes of Manasseh and Issachar, is truly blessed with the gifts of the heavens above and the springs below. No wonder that when Galilee is mentioned it is always with the definite article *the* before it. The Galilee, meaning *The Circle* is freely translated *The Region.* As Jesus *leads the way* over the Jordan, He enters *The Region* of the Promised Land... a paradise! *Deut. 33:13-17*

chapter two

The Wine Flows

As Scythopolis is approached, the other side of the Galilee impresses itself, "the Galilee of the Nations." From the beginning, the People of God who settled here have been completely dominated by their pagan neighbors. In fact, Scythopolis' territory is a spearhead of the pagan, Greek-oriented Decapolis thrust into the Galilee's side. Moreover, this city is its capital. To proclaim their complete domination, the pagans renamed the city (formerly called Bethshan) Scythopolis, after the famous Scythian warriors from the east thought to have invaded the country shortly before the exile to Babylon.

Tradition further relates that several centuries later these pagans were settled here by Alexander the Great during his attempt to conquer India. This eastern origin is also recalled in the worship in Scythopolis. They claim that Dionysus, the only god to be born of the union of their chief god Zeus and a human, stayed here during his journey from India to the west. As he traveled to Greece, demonstrating the art of cultivating the vine and bringing the blessing of wine to all along his way, his beloved nurse died. Her burial in Scythopolis gave a second pagan name to the city, Nysa.

The temple of Dionysus the wine god rests high above this sprawling city on the central acropolis. This hill contains the whole history of the city for it is composed of the ruined layers of all Scythopolis' predecessors. Dionysus was credited by these misguided people with producing the blessed paradise of this March morning. Dionysus, or Bacchus as he is also called, is for them the god of the life-giving vine and the spirit-imparting wine. Many residents of Scythopolis see him represented in the luxuriant vines laid out in rows about the city. The yearly cycle of the vine recalls his victory over tragedy and death.

Left:
The region of the blessed Galilee in bloom.

Below:
Dionysus, or Bacchus, as he is also called, the god of the life-giving vine and the spirit-imparting wine.

29

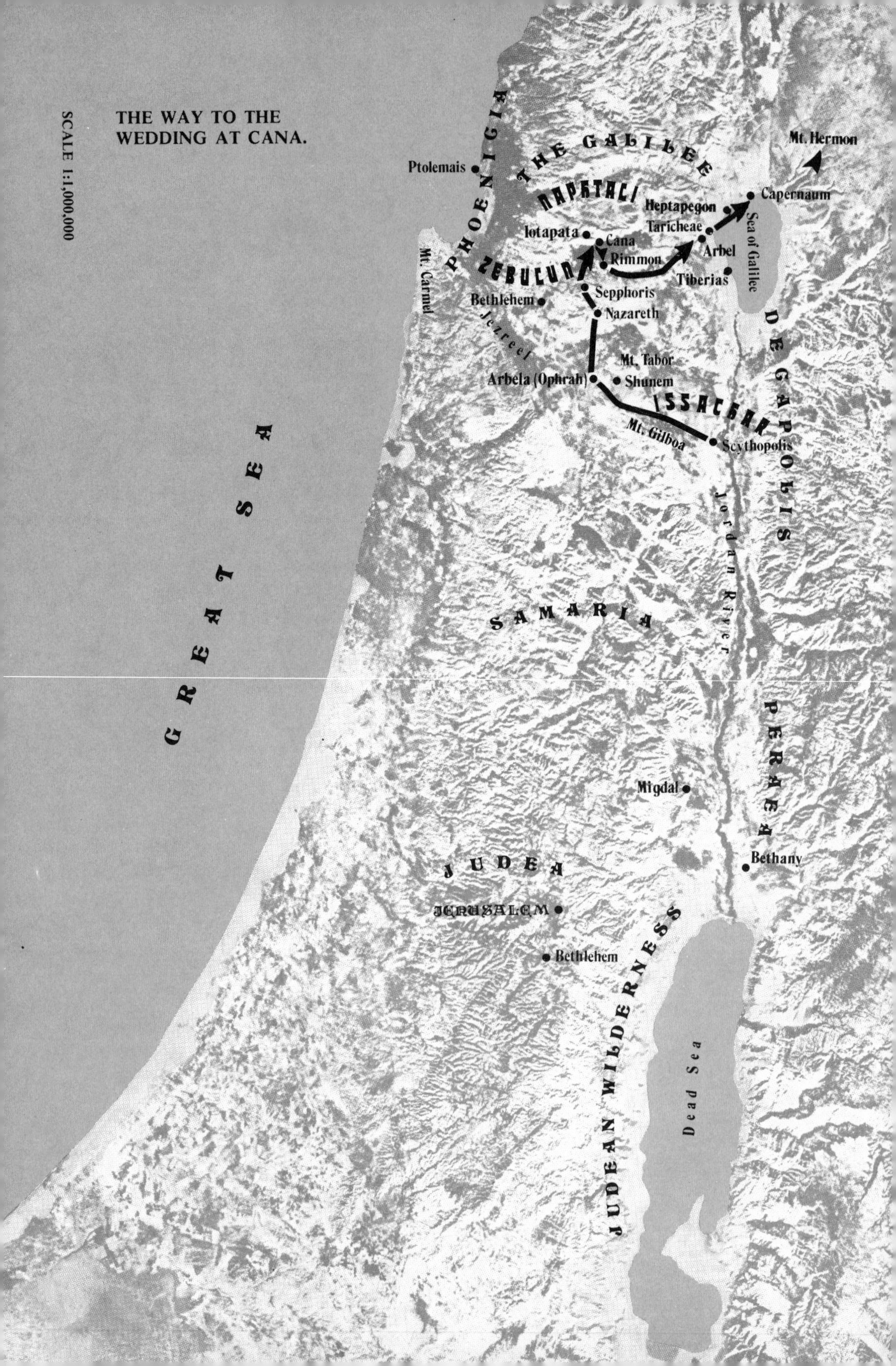

THE WAY TO THE
WEDDING AT CANA.

SCALE 1:1,000,000

GREAT SEA

PHOENICIA

THE GALILEE

NAPHTALI

Mt. Hermon

Ptolemais

Capernaum

Heptapegon

Iotapata   Taricheae

Cana   Sea of Galilee

Rimmon   Arbel

ZEBULUN

Mt. Carmel

Bethlehem   Sepphoris   Tiberias

Jezreel   Nazareth

Mt. Tabor

Arbela (Ophrah)   Shunem

ISSACHAR

Mt. Gilboa   Scythopolis

DECAPOLIS

Jordan River

SAMARIA

PERAEA

Migdal

Bethany

JUDEA

JERUSALEM

Bethlehem

JUDEAN WILDERNESS

Dead Sea

Each winter the vine has its branches pruned, leaving it a dismembered stump which appears hopelessly lost and dead. Such was the horrible death of the wine god himself. He became the object of the jealousy of Zeus' wife and was torn limb from limb! Yet death could not hold Dionysus (so claim his followers) any more than the cold, dark days of winter can keep the gnarled stump from again putting forth life as the warm days of spring begin. He is the only pagan god to defy death. In spring, the pagans rejoice that the vines about the city put forth their green shoots of new life which will bear much fruit by autumn. This sign is their hope of victory over death and for union with the gods. When they drink the wine of Dionysus, they feel they have become as a god, being at one with him. So wondrous is the blessing of Dionysus that some of his followers even claim that water is turned to wine on his feast day at his great temple in the west. No wonder that along with Asclepius, the god of healing, Dionysus is so popular among the pagans!

Jesus' disciples notice the People of God gathered in their communities in and about Scythopolis and realize how easily they can be ensnared by the pagan life. Throughout the history of God's People in the blessed Galilee runs the tragic tale of generation after generation turning from the Creator and worshipping His

Mount Tabor rises above the plain of Jezreel.

31

creation in forms of fertility gods like Dionysus in imitation of their neighbors. They forget so easily what the name of the valley through which the disciples now pass, Jezreel, *God Sows,* proclaims to all in the Galilee.

Jesus continues west through the broad valley passing through the territory of the former tribe of Issachar, blanketed with the finest wheat the Promised Land can produce. The history of this tribe reflects plainly the threat of paganism. Jacob, in his blessing of the tribes, compared the people of Issachar to a donkey who, seeing how pleasant this land is, willingly bowed his back to slave labor. The great powers who would subjugate God's People still control Issachar, be it the part under the control of the Decapolis or that under Herod Antipas who has been appointed tetrarch of the Galilee by Rome.

Gen. 49:14-15

The sweet smell of spring masks any bitterness as they continue toward Nazareth, moving along under the hump-shaped Mount Moreh. The village of Shunem on Moreh's slopes reminds one of the only Power Who can truly bring life from death. Elisha once showed that Power to this village during a grain harvest when the only son of an elderly woman was raised from the dead.

2 Kings 4:8-37

Soon they reach Arbela, the central village in the Plain of Jezreel, which was once called Ophrah. This was the hometown of Gideon, a mighty warrior of the People. God used Gideon to bring new life to the Galilee as he defeated the pagan forces. To be sure, it was not his might that led to that victory over the nations who dominated this rich plain. He was simply an instrument in God's hand. Through Gideon God demonstrated that with only a handful of His People, He could bring into subjection the unbelieving nations.

Judg. 6:33-8:3

As Jesus leaves Arbela and turns north toward the foothills of the lower Galilee, Mount Tabor comes into view, towering over the fields to His right. Its 1,500-foot height is accented by the flat northern finger of the Jezreel Plain which extends to its base. In its own way Mount Tabor also proclaims that *God Sows,* and *not* some fertility god. Crowned with a thick oak forest which is a sanctuary for wild life, it rises as another attestation of the goodness of God's creation.

In this area, God had once saved His People. This He did, not by the most modern of weapons of the best of horsepower, but rather by an abundance of that which those in southern Judea scarcely get enough — *rain!* Here Deborah gathered and Barak led the People against the mighty forces of the world. They faced sure defeat until it rained and rained, turning the dark brown fields of the Jezreel into a sea of mud through which the pagan army could not move and in which its chariots became stuck. Victory was easily won. The thoughts of the disciples might well be on such a possibility of victory despite seemingly hopeless odds as their small band leaves Jezreel's sprawling grain fields and starts up the steep, rocky approach to Nazareth, the humble hometown of their new Rabbi.

Judg. 4:1-5:31

Nazareth of the Galilee seems an odd place from which to expect a warrior king or an anointed one to emerge. Perhaps it is as odd a place for building dreams as that tiny farm village in Judea called Bethlehem, from which came the great king David! Nazareth does not lie at the top of the ridge overlooking the plain in a position for defense or control. Rather, after the tiring climb up the winding path to the top of the ridge, aching legs must still carry the travelers at least another twenty minutes before the comforts of the village are reached. After approaching the village by a slight rise, even in the fast-gathering darkness, its

Huddled under a steep, wooded hill, Nazareth is only a small cluster of houses gathered around a humble, gently flowing spring.

small extent can be completely seen at a glance. Nazareth is disappointingly small, hardly noticeable until one is in it. Huddled under a steep, wooded hill, it is only a small cluster of homes gathered around a humble, gently flowing spring. How appropriate its name, *Sprout!*

As night begins to fall at the end of this second long day of travel from Bethany of Peraea, dim lamp lights are gradually being extinguished as this farm village gets ready early for bed. After a good home-cooked meal, sleep comes easily in the coolness of the hill-sheltered village. The night air is permeated with the smell of pine and the silence is broken only by the rustle of wind through trees. The chirping of a lonely cricket provides an appropriately simple lullaby.

The next morning brings much excitement. There is an invitation to a wedding in Nathanael's hometown, Cana. Jesus, His mother, and disciples head over there on their third day of travel from Bethany of Peraea. Leaving cozy *Sprout,* they climb the path behind the village, kept pleasantly cool in the early morning by the shadow of hill and trees. Their climb is rewarded at the top as the world of the Galilee lies in front of them — from Mount Carmel in the south to snow-covered Mount Hermon looming far to the north. To their left the wooded hills of Zebulun roll down to meet the western end of the Plain of Jezreel whose eastern half they traversed yesterday.

John 21:2

JOHN 2:1

Bethlehem of the Galilee can be seen in the foothills overlooking the Plain of Jezreel, which is the land's breadbasket. The village's name, *Place of Bread,* seems more appropriate here in the north than for its sister village in Judea in the south. Behind Bethlehem and at the end of the Plain of Jezreel rises the Carmel

Mt. Carmel.

range running in a long majestic line to the sea. Its name is popularly understood to mean *Vineyard of God.* This is a good reminder that grapes are as abundant in the Galilee as in Judea. Just as nature and the vine are worshipped today at Scythopolis at the eastern end of the Plain of Jezreel, so this wooded mountain range overlooking the western entrance to the great plain has ensnared the People in ages past. In the morning light one can clearly see the high peak on Carmel's eastern end. Here Elijah in his contest with the priests of the nature gods, Baal and Asherah, demonstrated that the land's blessings come from the Creator alone. It is *God's Vineyard* and *God's Sowing,* Carmel and Jezreel, that He Himself waters to bring forth wine and bread.

1 Kings 18:17-40

Cana is in the distance in front of them. The huge Asochis Plain, called in Hebrew the Plain of Beth Netopha after the fine olives in the area, lies in front of the village. The first half of the plain to the left of Cana is filled with dark green squares of maturing grain. The other half, on Cana's right side, is still covered with water accumulated during the heavy winter rains which so bless the Galilee. The poor drainage of the Plain of Asochis has caused the formation of this shallow reservoir and is responsible for the reeds growing there. Cana, *Reed,* is named after these water-loving plants. When this part of the plain dries out later this spring, there will be enough moisture for late plantings, thus keeping the Asochis in constant production. This plain is but an introduction to the riches of the former tribe of Naphtali. The tribe's territory stretches behind the plain up to the mountains of the upper Galilee and sweeps from the plain's end down to the Sea of Galilee.

Continuing on their way to Cana, they descend over the pine and olive-covered hills of the former tribe of Zebulun. Where the trees leave off, terraces of grapes take over. Hence the village on the hill to their right is called Gathhepher. Gath means *press* and hepher, *well.* Wine flowing from presses where an abundant supply of water is drawn from wells — that name nicely captures the blessings of the Galilee. However, the importance of this village for the North is not its fine wine, but rather its prophet. This is the hometown of Jonah whose grave the Galileans often visit. The half-pagan Sepphoris dominates the view ahead of the disciples, and the heathen Phoenician coast glitters in the distance. They are reminded that through a Jonah, God had shown His concern for the pagans, engendering their repentance and belief in Him. In spite of the Judeans' boasting of the prophets who came from their midst, the North has produced its share of spokesmen for the faith. Elisha, Elijah, and Jonah had not only criticized the People but were concerned for the pagans who dominate this region as well.

2 Kings 14:25

Below Gathhepher, Rimmon, *Pomegranate,* sits under the narrow end of the long Mount Turan which forms the south side of the Asochis Plain. Its namesake grows in abundance in the area and is a special sign of God's blessing of fertility. It is filled with hundreds of juicy red seeds. No wonder the pomegranate was carried back by the spies sent out by Moses as a sign of the fertility of the land. To this day this fruit is depicted on the seven-branched lampstand in the Temple as if to say that the tree of light represents a tree of life. How appropriately the Song of Solomon mentions the juice of the pomegranate and wine as the lover's drink. Both are symbols of the hope of the final paradise to come.

Num. 13:21-23

Song 8:2

Sepphoris seems to grow ever larger as Jesus and the disciples approach it. Until recently it was the capital of the Galilee and still is a bustling city. Its size, however, does not spoil the beauty of spring's fullness which almost engulfs the city as it raises its head above the woods and fields. Its name, *Bird,* points to the constant swirling of nature above its well-watered lands. The city is economically dependent on the farmers who come to buy their seed or to ship the beautiful produce of their lands. Here, in turn, they can secure the luxuries from abroad imported through the coastal city of Ptolemais with which Sepphoris has a direct link.

As the city is approached, the combination of the smell of recently cut grass and the thick pine wood, the sight of milk cows contentedly grazing in the

A view over the plain of Beth Netopha, from the bustling city of Sepphoris.

37

pastures, the freshness of the first tiny, greenish-white blossoms starting on the olive, the large fiery-red flowers of the pomegranate, the expanse of the long green grain fields with grapevines beginning to put forth dots of green by their side, the flocks of birds hovering over this parade of nature, excites one and lightens the step. How unlike dry, desolate Judea is this place!

The village names seem to echo the praise of the Creator as they are called off by the traveler: *Bird* (Sepphoris), *Place of Bread* (Bethlehem), *Pomegranate* (Rimmon), *Press by the Well* (Gaththepher), *Sprout* (Nazareth) just left behind, and *Reed* (Cana) ahead. These are complemented by the names of the hills and plains on which they rest: *God Sows* (Jezreel), *Place of the Netopha Olive* (Beth Netopha), and *God's Vineyard* (Carmel). All are watched over in the far distance by the snow-capped *Sanctuary* (Mount Hermon).

As the road leading into Sepphoris is reached, the personal, friendly greetings of the farmers coming to town indicate how well the new Rabbi knows this territory. Sepphoris may have been recently declared the second city in the Galilee, since Tiberias by the Sea of Galilee became its capital a decade ago. However, it has not lost any of the life which makes it in truth still the Galilee's first city. Sepphoris' location is ideal not only for a trade center but also for political control. Rome's most difficult problem in this region is the resistance movement. Perhaps this is a result of the Galilee's abundant natural resources and the desire of its residents to fully control the wealth they produce. It may also be caused by the fighting spirit nurtured in a People who must live as second-class citizens. Rome's term for these freedom fighters is *bandits* whom they constantly attempt to weed out so that Galilee might know the "true peace" which only Rome can give. These bearers of peace in full battle dress patrol the streets of Sepphoris. Some of the new followers of Jesus cringe at the presence of the military and move on quickly to avoid possible detainment. Sepphoris stands in the center of the lower Galilee as a reminder to the surrounding villages that the true paradise of spring is yet to come. They wait for the wedding of God with His People which will bring His peace to the land where an occupation force now rules. Sepphoris is left behind and the way through the grain fields leading to Cana is taken with hope that soon the paradisaical wine will flow at the wedding of God and His People.

By noon they reach the hillock of Cana. It is located in the center of the north side of the Plain of Asochis, protected by the hills rising behind it. As it is approached, only a few of Cana's homes are visible on its top. The steep side facing the plain has been left bare, providing natural protection for the village. However, as the disciples climb the winding path which leads along the side of the hill, they see the village spread out between the high hills behind it and the ridge overlooking the plain in front.

Cana is very much a village of the People of God. Its population longs to break the foreign domination of places like Sepphoris which looms threateningly in the distance across the plain. The villages half-hidden in the hills above Cana harbor similar feelings. In fact, the valley leading into the hills behind Cana ends at a town called Iotapata which supports freedom fighters. Well-protected by the hills from any Roman invasion and built on a lower hill within a circle of higher hills, Iotapata might someday be an excellent command center and place of

John 6:42

Is. 62:4-5

Amos 9:13-15

Josephus, War III, 158-160

38

Above:
The villages' names
seem to echo the
praise of the Creator
as they are called
off by the traveler,
such as Bird
(Sepphoris)

The pomegranate
grows in abundance
all over the Galilee.
It is filled with
hundreds of juicy
red seeds.

refuge in an all-out war with Rome. It is difficult to imagine that even Rome's well-trained forces could ever take that town above Cana.

Dreams of revolution or nightmares of Roman domination and thoughts of the impending hard labor of the grain harvest are forgotten for the moment in a village which is rollicking in the midst of a week-long wedding festival. This is a fine time of year for fun and relaxation. The fields still must dry out before they can be harvested, the fruit trees are plowed, and the grapevines after careful pruning are now beginning to put forth new branches. All indications point to a good fall harvest and plenty of new wine "to enjoy". Actually, the guests have been enjoying the past year's labor in the vineyards as they toast the bride and groom again and again. As the wine is sipped and the dreams of paradise recalled, the budding grapevines about Cana seem to pale in comparison to those of the last days that some of the rabbis have promised:

2 Baruch 29:3, 5-6

And it shall come to pass; when all is accomplished
that was to come to pass in those parts, that the
Annointed One shall then begin to be revealed....
The earth also shall yield its fruit ten
thousandfold, and on each vine there shall be a
thousand branches, and each branch shall produce
a thousand clusters, and each cluster produce
a thousand grapes and each grape produce 120
gallons of wine!

JOHN 2:2-4 // How far in the future that day must be is noted as the last of the wine jars is emptied. When Jesus, His mother, and disciples arrive, the marriage feast is about to be spoiled. Jesus' mother takes Him aside in the courtyard of the home and asks that He somehow prevent any embarrassment to these friends. Perhaps He could go with some of the disciples over to Rimmon or up to Iotapata and buy some more of that all-important wedding refreshment. Jesus' response is totally unexpected. "Woman, what do your concerns have to do with Me?" In a small village of the Galilee where respect for elders is high, the words are doubly painful. This is the type of reply expected from some pagan's son in a city like Sepphoris, but to address one's mother as "woman" in a village of God's People is almost a verbal slap in the face. He does add the explanatory comment that His *hour* has not yet come. It is as if there is a specific time set for Him to act. Jesus makes it very clear that not even at His mother's bidding will He be forced to act before that *hour* which is appointed for the true wine to flow. After speaking in such a peculiar way, He does turn to solving the present wedding's crisis, but in a way no one could have expected.

JOHN 2:5-11 Since they are of God's People, the family has stone jars reserved for the various purifications prescribed by Moses. Stone jars are preferred for storing the purification water because they are easier to clean and free from cracks into which impurities easily settle... always a possibility when pottery jars are employed. In the Galilee fine basalt rocks are plentiful and can be shaped into beautiful black vessels which are nonpermeable. There are six such jars gathered in the courtyard. They are of no mean size, each reaching to the waist of the waiters who have been asked to fill them to the brim. Since there are no springs near Cana, each home must have cisterns in its courtyard. It takes time for the waiters to fill them with over 120 gallons of this cistern water! Their task completed, they are then asked to carry some of this water to the headwaiter. A wonder occurs. The headwaiter does not taste cistern water, but the finest of wines! He jokes with the bridegroom, not realizing the wine's Source, that everyone serves the good wine first when the guests can fully appreciate its beautiful bouquet, and later when they have drunk freely and are incapable of such fine discriminations, the cheap wine. However, the best wine has been kept until now. With this unexpected gift of 120 gallons of wine, the wedding has a most happy ending.

The winding path which leads along the side of the hill toward Cana.

Cana

Gen. 49:11-12

Amos 9:13

When the disciples learn the origin of this good wine, they are filled with even more excitement. To be sure, the wine is flowing in the Galilee, far from a Judah lauded for its grapes. Judah might be pictured with his clothing drenched in the blood of the grapes and his eyes reddened from wine. There the wine of paradise would flow. Yet here in former Israel the wine flows and a hill drips with it. The sign seems to be given which opens a window into the future of what this Jesus will bring. Could He not be the One to restore the fortunes of Israel? Could this wine at the wedding signal the coming of the final wedding of God and His People? Jesus again shatters expectations. The sign is not given in Judah which waits for its dry, rocky hillsides to produce abundant wine. How perfect is this place for the first sign of His power. It appears in the Galilean spring when all the signs of a paradise to come are surrounding any viewers who will just open their eyes and hearts to receive them.

The disciples begin to place complete trust in Jesus. They surmise that they must only wait for the consummation of this Sign-giver's time, Who began His ministry just one week ago. It has been like the first week of a New Creation. This true Wine-giver has shown by a sign of the Creator's presence His superiority to the wine god, Dionysus. Jesus is greater than any god-man of the Greeks or Romans. *He is the fulfillment of the hopes of the prophets who promised a New Creation.*

Right:
Plunging into the Sea of Galilee, Mount Arbel was split open in prehistoric times, left with a cut through which travelers can pass to the lake.

Horns of Hittin, a hill whose eroded sides give the impression of horns.

42

The easy day's journey down to Capernaum is one of rejoicing in the Galilean spring. After crossing the Plain of Asochis and passing through Rimmon, they turn east and travel along the broad way leading between the hills. After a two-and-a-half-hour walk, the grain fields suddenly fall away. Far below the deep blue of the Sea of Galilee appears. Their destination, the village of Capernaum, is easily recognized in the middle of the lake's north shore. As they start their descent to the lake, they pass the Horns of Hittin, a hill whose eroded sides give the impression of horns. Below, they reach the black, volcanically enriched fields on the flat top of Mount Arbel. This mount plunges into the Sea of Galilee. One of the many earthquakes in prehistoric times split it open, leaving a cut through which travelers can reach the lake. The village of Arbel is located

The steep side of Mount Arbel sweeps up from the end of the Gennesaret Plain.

where the path begins its winding descent into this deep crack. The way is not easy. After negotiating the descending switchbacks, one is forced to make several crossings of a small brook as it works its way to the lake through the narrow valley floor. Scores of openings line the sides of the cliff in the middle of the pass. The only access to them is by a narrow pathway cut in the face of the cliff. These caves have served as a refuge for many freedom fighters. The Romans and Herodians have often driven out these bandits, only to have these freedom fighters quickly return to this sanctuary.

Josephus, War
I, 304-313

Soon the Plain of Gennesaret is reached. Although not nearly as large as the Plain of Jezreel, it is the most productive plain in the Galilee. It begins at Magdala which is located under Mount Arbel and stretches around the lake to the north shore. At Magdala, also called Taricheae, Jesus and the disciples can eat lunch. Fish is always excellently prepared here. After lunch it takes only an hour to cross the Gennesaret Plain and reach the village of the same name. Originally Gennesaret was located on the top of the hill rising behind the present-day village. Its ruins appear like a huge pile of dirt dumped on the hilltop. Today the village is able to enjoy a place on the plain itself because of Rome's "peace." The harbor for Gennesaret is nearby, opening onto the part of the lake which bulges to give it the shape of a *harp* which is the meaning of Gennesaret.

Josephus, War
III, 516-521

Walking along the shore under the hill of ancient Gennesaret, they come to the area of Heptapegon, Greek for *Seven Springs*. It is a paradise within a paradise. Here an abundance of springs not only produces a jungle of life, but pours their mineral-rich water into aqueducts which irrigate nearby plains. Some are warm, helping to attract fish to this part of the lake. The lake is not deep here and is excellent for the use of dragnets. The fishermen in Jesus' band have reached home. They greet their friends who are preparing for the coming evening of fishing by the small harbor with its familiar steps cut in the natural rock. They begin to tell of the Rabbi who accompanies them and of a *fantastic wedding where as never before wine flowed.*

Josephus, War
III, 506-515

chapter three

The True Sanctuary in Judea

Early April marks the last burst of spring and the gradual ending of the fishing season. Since the Judean and Samaritan Passovers come rather late this year, there is an opportunity to attend the festival in Jerusalem or on Mount Gerizim without interrupting the fishing. Not everyone, of course, can afford to go up to Jerusalem or Mount Gerizim at this time. Some will have to remain to watch over the flocks that graze on the hills around the lake. During the dry hot months before the fish begin biting again in November, many fishermen will become shepherds, the perfect matching seasonal work in the Galilee. As the fields become less supportive of the flocks, the older sheep will gradually be taken to market until only those able to produce for the coming year will be left. The fishing season then will begin again. That thinning-out process has already begun in April as the tender, first-born lambs are taken for Passover.

To be in Jerusalem in time to celebrate Passover, Jesus and His newly-formed flock cannot spend much time in Capernaum. Of course, there is enough time for Philip, Andrew, and Peter to visit their hometown of Bethsaida, an easy twenty-minute walk from Capernaum. These few days are spent sharing what they have seen and heard from the new Rabbi. Their families agree that He is a teacher worth following. Who knows, He might even be the awaited anointed one! If He should become a king, just think what being part of His inner circle would mean for the future success of the already profitable fishing business. No longer would they be forced to pay taxes to Rome or lose all that money paid to the tax collector above or under the table for fishing licenses.

JOHN 2:12

With the blessings of family and friends, they follow Jesus to the Passover celebration, taking the easiest route from Capernaum up to Jerusalem, across the lake and through the Jordan Valley. As they cross from the northern to the southern shore in their small boat, Magdala is the first major village they see to starboard. The other name for this village is Taricheae, *Dried Fish*, an appropriate designation for this important fish processing center.

The fishing families of the Galilee, like the Zebedees, are solid upper middle class or even upper class citizens. They have a hand in one of the country's most lucrative export industries. Some of Jesus' followers will be able to give ample financial support for His recently inaugurated ministry.

Midway in the crossing, the cities off port and starboard witness to another aspect of life in the North. On the port side is Hippus, one of the prosperous Decapolis cities and a standard-bearer of Roman values. It serves as part of the defense system of Rome's eastern border. Tiberias, on the starboard side, was recently founded by Herod Antipas, tetrarch of the Galilee and Peraea and lackey of Rome. Set up as a center for Roman control of the eastern Galilee and

Left:
The Yarmuk
River

made the new capital of the North, this herald of Caesar's name is loathsome to the Galilean revolutionaries, some of whom are certainly on the boat with Jesus. These pro-Roman cities represent only too well the drain on the fishermen's fine income. They pray for an anointed one who will free the land from Tiberius Caesar's strong bonds, as God at the first Passover freed the People from Pharaoh.

Late in the morning the boat arrives at the southern shore, the territory of Gadara. This huge city of the Decapolis, located high above the valley's east side, stands guard over the Yarmuk River, known to the Greeks as Hieromyces. Its own rich territory lies between the river and the lake. The way through the Gadara part of the Jordan Valley is aptly described by the name of the first village they pass, Kefar Semah, *Growth Village*. All about them is the profusion of spring fruit. The Jordan River produces luxuriant plant life in its wide inner valley, creating a striking contrast to the barren chalk hills through which it cuts in the south. As they travel, they stay on the east side of the valley. Thus they will not have to cross the snaking Jordan River until they reach the ford near Jericho. In some of the villages through which they pass, Greek is spoken — a constant reminder that their way is outside of the Promised Land.

As the first day of travel ends in the territory of Pella across from Scythopolis, the setting sun turns the fields of early-ripening barley to shiny gold. Barley fields ready for harvest will be seen all the way to Jerusalem. It can be grown in the rocky soil of the Judean and Samaritan highlands as well as in these rich plains. Since the grain is much cheaper than wheat and very nutritious, it is common fare. However, it is not commonness that gives barley an important symbolic meaning at Passover, but rather that it is the first grain to be harvested in spring. This is a sign that God's blessing of rain in winter has brought forth sustenance for the dry months and that dreaded famine will pass over the People.

Lev. 23:9-14

Pilgrims attending the Passover Feasts in Samaria and Judea, therefore, carry the first harvested sheaves of barley to offer on the second day of Passover as a wave offering before the Lord. This will mark the beginining of the Feast of Unleavened Bread. By this offering of first fruit they acknowledge that the land is not theirs, but God's.

As the pilgrim-disciples begin their second day of travel, they observe many people at work in the fields. This is the reason Passover is not always the best attended of the great feasts celebrated in Jerusalem. The coming of the harvest and the ripening fruits and vegetables that must be tended mean that many farmers are not able to attend Passover every year. Succoth, the harvest festival in the fall, comes after all the crops are in, and is much more convenient to attend. Then there is time for relaxing before the winter rains begin. Of course, Judeans from Jerusalem never quite accept such an excuse from their brothers living in the North. They often deride them as "Galileans," lumping them together with the Samaritans and pagans.

The crossing of the Jordan River on the third day is anything but that of a conquering Joshua. Roman checkpoints control the entry of Jesus and His disciples into Judea. They then pass into the Jericho Plain, a part of Judea belonging to Caesar's family who received it as a gift from the Herodians. They were given a veritable gold mine. This is first indicated by the rows of palm trees

Josephus,War
I, 361

Above:
Barley is the first
grain to be
harvested in
Spring.

Left:
Pilgrims carry the
first harvested
sheaves of barley
to offer as wave
offering before the
Lord.

49

that line the way to Jericho. These huge groves are interrupted only by patches of thorn-like bushes called balsam, the base for a popular perfume. This is yet another source of wealth and tax revenue. No wonder Cleopatra once demanded this area as a present from her lover, Antony! No wonder Rome holds it tightly in hand. Here is truly a land befitting emperors!

Josephus,War
I, 407, 417

As the city of Jericho is approached, the palace built by Herod the Great and named after his mother, Cyprus, attracts the eye. Resting on a pinnacle overlooking the plains, the pure white palace complex is brilliantly illuminated by the early sun. This is a typically comfortable Roman lookout post that checks any advance from the east. Herod, like the Romans he imitated, made sure that the treasures of the plain would be protected with style. Imagine the haughtiness of building a bathhouse, complete with cool, medium warm, and steam bathing rooms, on the most inaccessible place above Jericho—even above the main palace itself! The backbreaking labor demanded of slaves and servants to haul water, fuel, and refreshments so that the oppressors of the country and their puppets might carry on their harsh suppression at luxurious ease is incredible.

Wealth also flows into Jericho from those who come in winter to sunbathe and luxuriate in its fragrance and warmth. This winter playground for the wealthy lies on the north side of the road to Jerusalem. It is dominated by the roadside palace whose white marble staircase leads down to a long, narrow pool that reflects the hanging gardens and statuary above it. Here the rich partake of

Cyprus

road to Jerusalem   Jericho

As the city of
Jericho is
approached,
Cyprus attracts
the eye.

50

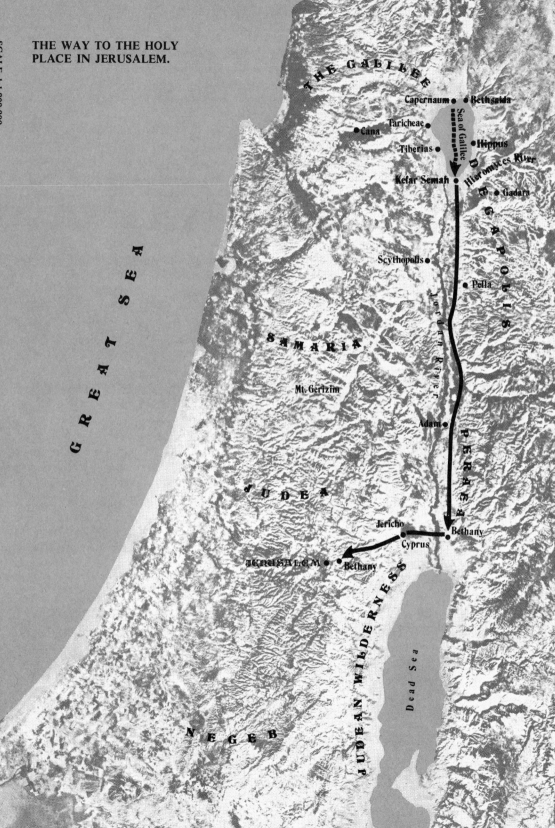

THE WAY TO THE HOLY
PLACE IN JERUSALEM.

SCALE 1:1,000,000

THE GALILEE

Capernaum ● ● Bethsaida

Cana ● Taricheae ●

Tiberias ● Sea of Galilee

Hippus ●

Kefar Semah ● Hieromyces River

DECAPOLIS

● Gadara

Scythopolis ●

● Pella

SAMARIA

Mt. Gerizim

PERAEA

Adam ●

JUDEA

Jericho ● ● Bethany

Cyprus

JERUSALEM ● ● Bethany

GREAT SEA

Dead Sea

JUDEAN WILDERNESS

NEGEB

Jordan River

the fruits of the labor of others. They lounge under the shaded porticoes or swim in the pools fed by an aqueduct that brings fresh spring water from the valley emerging from the Judean hills. Across this valley and facing the gardens is the great bath of Jericho. Here the sportsman, after exercising in the gymnasium, or a morning of hunting, can find a refreshing massage with perfume-spiced olive oil. He can also carry on business in its shaded porches. Theater and stadium events are also provided to prevent any boredom.

To the north, beyond the playground of the wealthy, the other face of Jericho is seen in row after row of small, mud brick houses. These are the homes of those whose toil makes the palm and balsam yield their riches. They cater to the wishes of the winter crowds who arrive after the date harvest and the oppressive heat of the summer. The dream of these people is of an anointed one who will lead the way to Jerusalem at the great and final Passover and end their toil and servitude. The words of the first psalm of the Hallel to be sung at the beginning of the Passover meal express their hope proclaiming that God "raises the poor from the dust, and lifts the needy from the ash heap to make them sit with Princes."

The way to Jerusalem can be very tiring in April if the sky is cloudless, allowing the scorching sun full reign. As one struggles up the steep, desert hills of the first half of the way, the words of the second Hallel refresh and encourage. Not only will the poor be made rich at the last Passover, but these barren hills

The city appears below the Mount of Olives.

will become part of the awaited paradise as the Lord "turns the rock into a pool of water, the flint into a spring of water." That wonder is underscored by the aqueduct on the side of the valley below the road. A green line appears on the barren hillside where water seeps out of its cracks.

About halfway up to Jerusalem, the pilgrims come to a strategically placed rest station. From here they have their first view of the Mount of Olives. Pilgrim bands can be seen along the way heading to God's House on the other side of the mount. Of course, there are also Roman troops along the way as well as at this inn. At the final Passover the occupation of these idolaters will be broken and their taunt, "Where is their God?" answered. In a few days the pilgrims will dream of this as they sing the third Hallel at the conclusion of the Passover meal.

Ps. 115

As the way draws closer to the Mount of Olives the number of pilgrims increases. Some lead their first-born lambs for the sacrifice. Others have barley tied to their sacks. The words of Passover's fourth Hallel ring out: "I will pay my vows to the Lord in the presence of all His People in the courts of the House of the Lord." The excitement of the festival procession uplifts and carries the weary travelers through the final part of the climb.

Ps. 116

As the last checkpoint is passed, the pilgrims begin to separate. Some go over the Mount of Olives to stay in Jerusalem or set up a camping place near the city. Others, like Jesus and the disciples, continue straight ahead to Bethany of Judea. All have the hope that one day the world will join the Passover throng in coming to the House of God as the fifth Hallel exhorts.

Ps. 117

On the next day, the disciples and their new Rabbi head toward Jerusalem. As the city appears below the Mount of Olives, the popular refrain of the Hallel sung not only at Passover in the spring, but also at Succoth in the fall is very much in mind.

Ps. 118

> *Hosanna!* Save us, we beseech Thee, O Lord!
> O Lord, we beseech Thee, give us success.
> Blessed be he who enters in the name of the Lord!
> We bless you from the House of the Lord.

Perhaps one day Jesus will come in triumphant fulfillment of that hope as He begins to reign in the Temple.

The city is entered with much excitement by the gate of the Essenes at the Pool of Siloam. The former City of David on the narrow hill rising above them, and his beautiful tomb not far from Siloam raise hopes for an anointed one like David. The steep way carries the pilgrim's gaze up to the high place where David bought a threshing floor to be used as foundation of God's Dwelling. The disciples walk in the footsteps of thousands of the faithful before them who have gone in joyous procession at that Holy Place. The Ascent Psalms which have been on the lips of those pilgrims through the ages, sum up the joy of being in the city of His earthly habitation.

1 Kings 2:10

2 Sam. 24:18-25

Ps. 120-134

As the middle of David's former city is reached, they marvel at the odd location of the tiny Jerusalem from the days of David to Nehemiah. This hill (Mount Zion) on which God's Dwelling rests is dominated by the surrounding hills. The explanation for this first location of Jerusalem is simple. The only spring in the area is at the base of this low hill. Its name is Gihon. The first Jerusalem and God's House were safe in

Overleaf:
The steep way carries the pilgrim's gaze up to the high place.

53

2 Sam. 5:6-10 this odd location, witnessed by the difficulty David had in taking it from the Jebusites. The Kidron Valley provided a moat on its eastern side as did the Tyropoeon Valley along its western and southern sides. This valley kept the steep and protective hills a safe distance from the city. The higher hills about Jerusalem, far from being threatening actually contributed to its security. So God would protect His People, as the Ascent Psalm reminds the pilgrim bands:

Ps. 125:2

> As the hills are round about Jerusalem,
> so the Lord is round about His People,
> from this time forth and for evermore.

The manner in which God can turn His whole creation to give security to His People causes a combination of awe and humility.

Josephus, War V, 184-227 That feeling of humility is heightened by the tremendous platform covering the Temple Mount which is now in full view, soaring above the ascending pilgrims. Herod the Great had raised this podium for God's earthly footstool in an almost superhuman building effort. Solomon's fabled preparations for the House of God pale beside it. Herod first built an enclosure wall over 128 feet high along the eastern side along the Kidron Valley. Then he built one of almost the same height over the Tyropoeon Valley on the west, and connected them with the southern wall to which the pilgrims now advance. Gigantic pieces of white limestone, some weighing up to 100 tons and reaching a length of 36 feet needed 1000 wagons (so it was claimed) in order to transport them from the quarries. Each was finely dressed with smooth-faced protruding centers, framed by perfectly even borders. By means of levers and pulleys operated more by human than animal power, they were set neatly in place to raise the platform to its dizzying height above the valley floors. Between the walls arched substructures were built. Finally, on the top of these the floor of the Temple area was laid in various patterns of stonework. It took eight and a half years to complete the platform alone! Indeed, some of the subterranean structures and the buildings set upon it are still not completed. Started in the eighteenth year of the reign of Herod the Great, the building of the Temple complex is now in its forty-sixth year.

John 2:20

The pilgrims first see the huge Royal Porch rising above the southern side of the platform. This is the largest of the four porches surrounding the Temple area. Its finely cut, gleaming white limestone blocks form a basilica style building with a high central roof. What a perfect facade for those ascending to view in anticipation of the splendor of the House hidden behind it! This grandeur, however, is checked by the monument to the prophetess Huldah located between the two entryways that lead to the Temple area above. Huldah had warned an overconfident Jerusalem that God's earthly dwelling would remain only so long as His People carry out His commandments, and so make this place worthy of His name.

2 Kings 22:14

The attention given to the Royal Porch is distracted by the magnificent, bustling market place in front of the Temple platform. It is filled with pilgrims and residents hurrying to complete their last-minute shopping for the feast. Stands are heaped with bitter herbs — various kinds of lettuce, dandelion, chicory

The feeling of humility is heightened by the tremendous platform covering the Temple Mount.

and endive — that will find their way to Passover tables. As they are eaten the bitterness of the captivity in Egypt will be remembered. The People will pray that God will remove the bitterness of the Roman occupation.

Fresh fruits are scarce at this time of year. Most of the fruits for sale were dried last fall. They include figs, dates, carobs, raisins and apricots. A variety of nuts is available also. The shoppers will mix the fruits and nuts into a paste seasoned with vinegar. During the Passover meal the bitter herbs will be dipped in this.

In the meat stalls, dressed lamb and the cheaper mutton from sheep no longer worth fattening or useful for bearing, hang from hooks. Some stall-keepers cover the meat with cloths to keep ever-present flies away. Here and there can be seen some beef for sale, but it is less popular and more expensive in Judea. Doves, as well as live sheep and cattle, are kept in enclosures either for home slaughter or for sacrifice on the altar in front of God's House.

Mingled with those selling food other vendors sell cloth, jars, lamps and various household necessities. Of course, never to be avoided are Jerusalem's souvenir hustlers with trinkets for visitors as reminders of their pilgrimage to the Holy City. The buying and selling in the holiday mood is infectious. Shouting and bargaining go on in the babel of tongues—Latin, Greek and a myriad of

57

They mount the monumental staircase behind the market place which leads to the Huldah Gates.

Ps. 133

Ps. 129:3-5

Aramaic dialects. In spite of the aggressiveness of the merchants... "You from Rome?" ... "I have a brother in Rome."... "Great city"... "Now I give you a special deal." ... "Oh, I know you can get this in Corinth, but really like this?"... "Think of your loved ones who deserve the best from *Jerusalem*." Through all this cacophony there emerges a feeling of what it means that God's People, no matter where they may have settled throughout the world, are united here at God's House on Mount Zion.

They rejoice with hundreds of the faithful who have increased Jerusalem's population fourfold for the festival as they mount the monumental staircase behind the market square. That joy, however, is momentarily broken when the doorway to one of the Huldah Gates is reached. Each of these double-doored entries leads to an underground passageway that brings the pilgrims up to the level of the Temple area. Here one must be checked by the ever-present soldiers who guard against any disturbance of the "peace" Rome has brought to Jerusalem. To ferret out any who would use the podium above as a rallying point for revolution, each pilgrim is forced to submit to a body search while all things carried up to the Holy Place are carefully examined. Objects like sticks and clubs which might easily be converted into weapons against Roman forces may not be carried past this point. As the pilgrims are allowed to proceed, they might well be mumbling the Ascent Psalm:

The plowers plowed upon my back;
they made long their furrows.
The Lord is righteous;
He has cut the cords of the wicked.
May all who hate Zion
be put to shame and turned backward!

Perhaps the affliction soon will be brought to an end. Perhaps the cord of
occupation will be snapped and those cords used in turn to drive out the
imperialistic oppressor. This is the hope of the pilgrims who move in the
semidarkness of the passageway leading to the light of the Temple at its end.

Suddenly the ascending steps cease and the pilgrims arrive at the massive
floor of the platform. Their gaze is carried across the expanse in front of them,
past the low-latticed fence built to prevent pagans from entering the most sacred
place on earth, up the twelve steps to the three gold-covered entry doors to the
Men's Court, and above the court's exquisite white walls to rest on the towering
Sanctuary behind. Its sides are of highly polished white limestone, perfectly cut
and fitted to give the impression of a sheet of marble. Plates of gold and silver
have been hung on them, combining with the glistening limestone to reflect the
morning sun so intensely that God's House becomes almost as difficult to gaze

Each Huldah
Gate leads to an
underground
passageway
which brings the
pilgrims up to the
level of the Temple
area.

59

upon as the sun itself. It is amazing that God's earthly Dwelling was basically finished after only a year and a half of intensive building. However, flourishes and hidden decorations are still being added which it seems only God can see. It is still not complete.

What can be seen of this light to the world is almost incomprehensible! Crowned with delicate golden spikes which keep birds away, preserving the building's purity, it is truly an earthly throne worthy of God. As the eyes gradually adjust to the first dazzling impression, they discern that the square front of the building is higher and much wider than the narrower and longer part

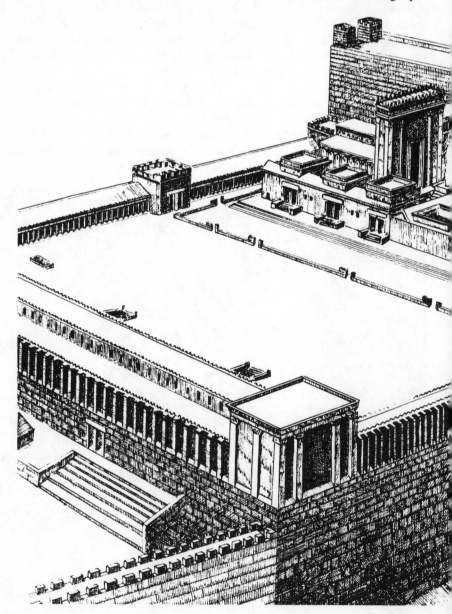

The Holy Place

behind it. This combination of a wide and high entry porch attached to the narrower and lower, but longer Holy Place and Holy of Holies, gives the impression of a stylized lion crouching, ready to attack any invader of God's House of Prayer. David truly brought a blessing to the People through his choice of this mount for God's footstool. *Ps. 132*

The double-columned, 44-foot-wide porches on the eastern and western sides of the Temple area almost casually catch the viewer's attention with their row upon row of fine, marble-like polished columns. Each is capped by a finely carved Corinthian capital which supports a cedar-paneled ceiling 37 feet high.

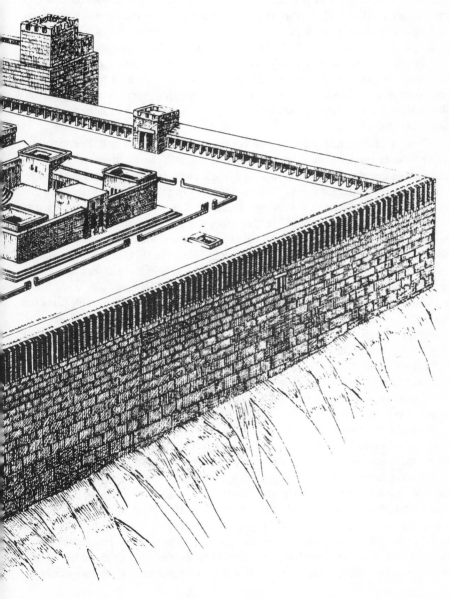

Josephus, War V, 238-245

Ps. 124

Among the crowd beneath, one notices that not only are the People of God taking in this scene, but also Roman soldiers on patrol. The earthly throne is anything but free. Behind the magnificent Seat of God stands a much larger Roman military stronghold named by Herod the Great for a pagan commander, the Antonia. The southeast turret of this barracks has been purposely raised high enough to allow for observation of all activity in the Sanctuary courts. Yet, even the raw might of the construction bearing down on God's House cannot fully detract from the Sanctuary's splendor. Nor can its presence be permanent.

As the disciples turn, following the line of porches around the Temple area, the portico under which they have just passed, the Royal Porch attracts their attention. This huge structure runs the entire 318-foot length of the south side of the Temple platform. It is supported by 160 polished marble columns, each one so large that three persons can barely join hands around its base. These are arranged in four rows, centered on the gigantic stairway leading down to the Tyropoeon Valley. The two lower parts of the ceiling have finely carved patterns in white limestone, while the higher, central portion is paneled with cedar. The combination of refreshing shade given by the soaring porch and the forest of glistening columns brings to a climax the sense of joy and blessedness of being near His Holy House.

The overwhelming mingling of hopes, dreams, visions and thankfulness, which vibrate through the Ascent Psalms, along with the greatness of structure and fineness of detail combine to sweep the viewer up in a crescendo of joy — shattered by a grating screech. "Come on ... I give you a special price for your Passover sacrifice," screams a raucous huckster. The smell also strikes in discord with the clean, polished pillars. The oxen strung along the porch ready to be sold as sacrifices mingle their defecation with that of lambs. Their lowing and bleating add to the chorus of yelling and screaming. Under a row of columns in the porch's semidarkness hover the collectors of the yearly half-shekel tax demanded of all God's People. It is paid not in quiet thankfulness, but with bitter accusations of gouging. There are loud complaints against unreasonable rates for currencies that pilgrims must exchange into the coinage required for the offerings. It hurts to see the poor peasants who have saved and sacrificed so that they might attend the feast being shortchanged by these abusers of the tithes for

Lev. 5:7

the maintenance of God's House. The pitiful cry of a poor man is heard in response to the price asked for a simple dove, which is the acceptable offering of those who cannot afford the required offerings of sheep or oxen. There is no show of pity by those who control the market.

JOHN 2:14-15
14-25

As the din rises in contrast to the majesty of the Royal Porch and sweeps over the courtyard to that glistening symbol of God's goodness, Jesus moves to where the cattle and sheep are tied. He picks up tethering cords made of rushes. These have been discarded as tied wicker baskets of doves were emptied. He quickly fashions them into a many-stranded scourge in defiance of the pagan rulers who allow no weapons in the Temple area. He begins to beat those selling the sheep and cattle. He unties the animals, driving them along with their owners toward the grand staircase exit at the end of the porch. As He moves along through the rows of columns, His feet kick at the low coin tables of the moneychangers while a free hand snatches at their purses to fling away their ill-gotten gains. The ring of the rolling coins, coupled with the cry of the animals and shrieks of the shocked merchants, causes everyone to freeze for a moment.

As He drives out the sellers of doves, He begins to explain His actions. These cheaters of the poor along with the other merchants are to get out of this place of worship and take their business to the markets below. Turning to God's beautiful Sanctuary, He makes their insults even more personal. He calls it His Father's House which they have dared to make into a house of trade, a mere emporium. The prophet's words are being fulfilled as the traders leave the Temple. This shock-filled moment will not be forgotten by Jesus' followers, for He also seems to fulfill the words of David himself: "Zeal for your House has consumed me." *JOHN 2:16-17* *Zech. 14:21* *Ps. 69:9*

The Judeans in charge of the Temple, reinforced by the Temple police, quickly recover from their astonishment. The Roman soldiers, to be sure, do not interfere and are probably even a bit pleased with the chaos and the mess left behind. One of the Judeans has done what they themselves had been so often tempted to do. Many Judeans will never forget this insult as the words of David begin to be further fulfilled: "It is for Your sake that I have born reproach, that shame has covered my face." *Ps. 69:7-8*

The Judean officials gathering about Him demand some explanation for His actions. Jesus' answer is provocative. He challenges them to destroy the Sanctuary so that in three days He can raise it. But all this magnificence could not be taken apart in three days let alone put together again! Could He accomplish in three days what has taken thousands of workers 46 years to build? How absurd! Later, Jesus' disciples will begin to understand that what is meant is not this building, but Jesus' very Body. He is the link between heaven and earth and not this structure, whose beauty people can so easily mar and whose sanctity desecrate. As the Passover comes and many begin to trust in Him, Jesus does not return the trust. He sees around Him, in the debris of the Royal Porch, what is in a human being. *JOHN 2:18-22* *JOHN 2:23-25*

Few understand this sign. Nicodemus, for one, a teacher in Jerusalem who visits Jesus during one of the nights of His sojourn here, cannot understand the new birth and life Jesus points toward. Perhaps His words are too much of a riddle. He directs Nicodemus' thoughts away from Jerusalem and back to the wandering in the desert after the first Passover. There a healing serpent was raised along the way to save a dying People. So will He be lifted up that those in Judea and the world might find life and forgiveness in the true Sanctuary now in Judea — His Body. *JOHN 3:1-21* *Num. 21:8-9*

Bethel's High Place

chapter four

The Wedding

The cleansing of the Temple was bound to cause repercussions. Nevertheless, it is not under extreme pressure that Jesus leaves Jerusalem in the beginning of May. That opposition will gradually build up in the next year and a half until the road north of Jerusalem, which He now travels at leisure, becomes His escape route. Now is a time to minister in Judea. This ministry does not necessarily move directly north of Jerusalem. Pilgrims from the Galilee often visit such places as Mamre and the tomb of the Patriarchs in Hebron. Finally, however, His ministry does move north toward Samaria. Many Judeans respond to Him and are baptized.

JOHN 3:22

Jesus walks in the footsteps of almost all the main figures of the Scriptures who have traveled this way. He first passes the famous villages of the former tribe of Benjamin, that southernmost tribe of Israel now taken over by Judea. The villages reflect the sad history of division among the People of God. Just north of Jerusalem are the ruins of Gibeah of Saul which remind the disciples of the failure of the first one to be hailed as king. This former center for the People is now a guard post for the hated Romans. Anathoth, the home of Jeremiah the Benjaminite critic of Judah, is not far from the road to the east. In the distance to the west, opposite Saul's village, rises the high place of Gibeon where his successor, David permitted the elimination of all but one of his heirs. It was also here that David's son, Solomon, had prayed for the wisdom which his successors finally rejected, splitting the kingdom in half. Gibeon itself lies to the north, below the high place. Although this village is a reminder of the victories of the first Joshua-Jesus, it is also the site of the fierce and decisive battle between the house of Benjamin's Saul and Judah's David. As the road north passes Ramah, the tragic results of that "victory" for the Judeans becomes clear. Here at Ramah the northern confederation, Israel, tried to recover the territory lost to Judah after the victory of David's house. But Judah, with the help of a pagan nation, pushed Israel farther north to Mizpah. That help was secured by plundering the treasures in God's House.

1 Sam. 10:20-11:7

Jer. 1:1-19

2 Sam. 21:1-14

1 Kings 3:3-15

Josh. 9:1-10:14

2 Sam. 2:12-17

1 Kings 15:16-22

The hill upon which the ruin of Mizpah lies is soon seen by the disciples, for it blocks the way north. This had been a great meeting place of the tribes where Samuel pronounced the Benjaminite Saul king of the People. Here, too, he warned them that such a move was a rejection of God as King. The disastrous result of the kingship and the divisions it caused are also remembered. After the destruction of Jerusalem, the remnant of Judah had gathered at Mizpah only to see a Judean kill his Israelite brothers who were on their way to mourn the destruction of God's House. This was immediately followed by Judean killing Judean as this torn remnant continued the struggle for power. After an hour's

1 Sam. 10:17-24

Jer. 40-41

Left:
The narrow valley leading to the large village of Bethel.

65

1 Kings 12:25-33

Gen 28:10-22

Josh. 16:1-2

Josephus, Antiquities XIII, 125-127

Against Apion II, 43

Josephus,War III, 48-51

John 2:23-24

The number of
evergreen olive
trees gracing the
hillsides suddenly
multiplies.

walk, Jesus and His followers climb through the narrow valley leading to the large village of Bethel. The Judeans once claimed that the Israelites set up idols on the high place behind the village where angels once ascended and descended on Jacob-Israel. This village was well inside Israel in the days of the Judges, and marked the border between Benjamin and Joseph, the central tribe of Israel. During the period of the divided kingdom, Bethel served as a border village of the North.

The movement of the Judeans past Bethel and into Ephraim, the southern part of Joseph's tribe, impresses with the extent of Judah's victory over Israel. With the support of the great pagan conqueror, Alexander the Great, several centuries ago, Judah succeeded in extending its territory north even past Shiloh. This forced the former Israelites, now called Samaritans, into the center of Joseph's inheritance around Mount Gerizim. That the Judeans have taken over territory far richer than their original land is soon evident as the number of evergreen olive trees gracing the hillsides suddenly multiplies. Where the soil of the hills becomes too rocky for planting, the valleys give the impression of wealth. In May, high stands of grain begin to turn a harvest-blond. To extend the boundary so far north and control it, much blood had been shed by the Judeans. No wonder Jesus does not trust them even though they claim to believe in Him.

A view to Mount
Gerizim from
Ebal.

Their ancestors achieved a hollow victory. Of this the disciples would be
constantly reminded as they pass Roman troops moving along the way south to
Jerusalem or north to Sebaste. The latter city now rests on the ruins of Israel's
former capital, Samaria, the name the remnant of Israel still bears. The king of
the Judeans, Herod the Great, changed the name. His choice of a name tells the
whole story of the state of the People of God, be they Samaritan or Judean.
Sebaste, meaning *August One,* is a title for the greatest Caesar, Octavian. His
successor, Tiberius, is the real triumphant power in the land. The pagan Caesar
dictates who can or cannot hold this or that territory and takes his percentage of
its produce. Near the frontier of Judea, just north of ancient Shiloh, the disciples
have their first view of Mount Gerizim which dominates Samaria. Below that
detested mount lies a Roman camp, a nagging reminder that the pagan occupiers
respect none of the divisions among the People of God. The camp is also a
warning that no more Judean attempts to destroy this corrupt offshoot of the
true religion will be tolerated.

The inhabitants of the villages nestled in the hills near the Samaritan plain to
which the disciples look, take exception to the typical Judean charge that they
are heterodox. The Samaritans would proudly point out that all the major events
of the People of God have taken place here in the center of what was once a far
larger Israel. Noah's ark landed on this holiest of mountains. Here Abraham
offered his son, Isaac. After the Exodus, the tribes carried twelve stones from the
Jordan River to this mount's top, setting them up as a remembrance of their
covenant with God. God had designated this mount especially for the offering of
sacrifices. The Samaritans wait on this day in May for a prophet to arise who

67

Gen. 14:18-20
(Samaritan
Version)

Gen. 33:18
(Samaritan
Version)

Hosea 1-3

JOHN 3:23-24

JOHN 3:25-36

Hosea 2:18-20

Josh. 24

will restore the former glory of this center. They also point with pride to the village of the Salim facing Mounts Gerizim and Ebal. This village is so important that Samaritans refer to it not merely as Salim, but rather *The* Salim. Here, they recall, the great priest-king Melchizedek received offerings from Father Abraham. It was here, too, that Abraham's grandson, Jacob, first stopped on his return after he married Laban's daughters.

Though Samaritans take pride in the great figures who graced the blessed richness of their land, they are also aware of the past failures of Israel-Samaria. The fertile hills and valleys have seduced them from time to time as they turned to worship that fertility. Hosea, their own prophet had called this harlotry. In times past, they had left God, their true *husband* (in Hebrew baal) for false *husbands*, baalim. The Judeans, of course, claim they still are joined to a false baal, having broken forever their wedding bond with the true God.

This May morning the voice of a prophet is still heard in Israel-Samaria. Just an easy three-quarters-of-an-hour walk downhill from the Salim the call for repentance is being made again. The promise of a new marriage of repentant People to their God is being proclaimed by none other than John the Baptist. Seeming to follow the season, he has moved from Bethany of Peraea to the region of Aenon. Aenon lies at the head of the broad entry valley to Samaria from the east. It is separated from the Salim by a mountain. Between this mountain and Mount Ebal, a deep cut was ripped open by an earthquake millions of years ago. This provided a main artery for travel from central Samaria north to Scythopolis and east to the ford across the Jordan River by ancient Adam. It is a heavily traveled thoroughfare much like the way past Bethany of Peraea.

Aenon is not a town, but rather an area below the cut into which many springs flow year round. In the heat of a May afternoon fields are white from drying wheat, and flowers and grass wither on the hills. Aenon presents a refreshing contrast with its green, shaded valley and cool springs. In fact, Aenon means *Springs*. This well-watered area provides the Baptist with a perfect second center for his work. As Judeans go to the area of the Jordan Valley to escape the chilling cold of winter, so Samaritans go to Aenon for relief from the stifling heat of summer. By mid-May the Jordan Valley can be unbearably hot. People no longer vacation in Jericho or Bethany of Peraea. John now has moved from there to a Samaritan holiday center. He addressed a predominately Judean crowd in Bethany, and here finds the opportunity to preach to Samaritans. Tensions between Samaritan and Judean are dissolved by this odd preacher of repentance.

His disciples, of course, include Samaritans. These, quite naturally, discuss with Judeans the baptisms being performed by Jesus' disciples not far away near the border of Judea and Samaria. John's response to their questions about Jesus is given in that marriage imagery which is so much a part of northern prophetic language. *The Bridegroom is coming*! John's task in Samaria is that of the friend who prepares the way for the Bridegroom. Jesus is about to enter Samaria and John's preparations are complete. He now can slowly move aside as the wedding is about to take place. He hears the Groom coming and focuses attention on the Plain of the Salim above Aenon which leads to the pass between Mounts Gerizim and Ebal. Here at the great crossroads of the country, the true center of the

Promised Land, the first Joshua-Jesus led in the covenant ceremony that united God and His People. Here the remnant of Israel awaits an anointed one.

Perhaps it is the slowly mounting opposition of the Pharisees in Judea that makes the entry into Samaria *necessary* as Jesus prepares to return to the Galilee. It could also be the *need* to avoid the long return route first to Bethel, and then north through the blistering hot Jordan Valley which must be followed to shun detested Samaritan territory. Maybe the harvest-time of a People prepared by John the Baptist for their renewed covenant of marriage makes it *necessary* at this time for Jesus to pass through Samaria on His way back to the Galilee. Most probably, however, the *necessity* is a result of the combination of all these forces at work on this clear, warm morning in late May when Jesus and the disciples set out early from Lebonah of Judea.

Lebonah is one of the last large villages where Judeans can rest at ease before crossing into Samaria. It is nestled at the bottom of the steep drop in the

Aenon presents a refreshing contrast with its green, shaded valley and cool springs.

JOHN 4:4

69

main road to Samaria. A rich valley extends north to the Samaritan border. In this valley, fields are tall with wheat ready for the harvest. The border is also a valley that crosses the one from Lebonah. This final border which Judah has made with Israel lies 23 miles north of the first boundary, the Hinnom Valley, on the south side of Jerusalem.

Jós. 15:8

After they pass the last Judean settlement, a road station called Anuathu Borcaeus, Jesus and His disciples cross the border-forming valley. There is a short climb up the Samaritan side of the valley until it suddenly drops off into the great central plain of the Samaritans. Mount Gerizim dominates the west side of this plain. A century and a half ago the Judean high priest, John Hyrcanus, tried to eliminate the false center of worship on this mount, leaving it in ruins. Just like the thorn that will not be eradicated from the sides of the beautiful grain fields under Mount Gerizim, this holy place quickly grew again into the center of Samaritan worship.

Josephus, War III, 51-52

Josephus, Antiquities XIII, 256

Following Jesus into the long plain leading toward Mount Gerizim, the disciples note the main cemetery of the Samaritans which dominates the east side of the plain. The Samaritans claim the first priests of Israel, the son and grandson of Aaron (Eleazar and Phinehas), are buried here. The graves of many Samaritan high priests are also in this village. The Samaritans aver that this is the Gibeah, *Hill,* of the Joshua account although now calling it Tirathana. Judeans scoff at such a claim. Gibeah, they assert, should not be located here in northern Ephraim, but rather in southern Ephraim inside Judean territory. Indeed, the "Mount Gerizim" across the valley from it is probably not the mount to which Joshua came after crossing the Jordan as the Samaritans claim. That mount is also inside Judean territory, towering over Jericho not far from Gilgal. These despicable people not only change geography at will, but even dare to tamper with the Scriptures to make them fit their territory! Although Moses wrote in his last book that the stones of witness should be set up on Mount *Ebal,* they even changed that to read "Gerizim" to make it refer to their present holy place. Similar tampering can be seen in the attempt to justify the claim that Melchizedek came from that Salim located in front of their holy mount. They have changed the account of Jacob's reentry into this area in the first book of Moses to read that Jacob came from Salim to Shechem, rather than as the Judeans correctly gave it, "Jacob came *safely* to the city of Shechem."

Josh. 24:33

Josephus, Antiquities XVIII, 85-89

Deut. 27:4

Gen. 33:18

The Judeans do not deny the presence of the great figures of the faith in this area. They remember that after Jacob came safely into this region, his daughter Dinah was raped near Shechem between Mounts Ebal and Gerizim. Rachel had buried her family gods at Shechem's holy place as if to leave this center forever defiled. In front of the ruins of Shechem there is a well by the road which Jesus and the disciples now approach. Here, it is claimed, Jacob refreshed himself and watered his cattle. The tradition seems odd, for less than 300 yards away flows a very accessible spring which provided water for ancient Shechem and now is the main source of water in the village of Balluta. The name of the village means *Oak* and recalls that Abraham worshiped under an oak at Shechem when he first entered Canaan. The Judeans, however, call the village Sychar, a derogatory name meaning *Drunkenness,* which sums up their opinion of the Samaritans. It is difficult for them to acknowledge the grave of another Patriarch, Joseph. This is

Gen. 33:18-34:31

John 4:6,12

Gen. 12:6-7

JOHN 4:5

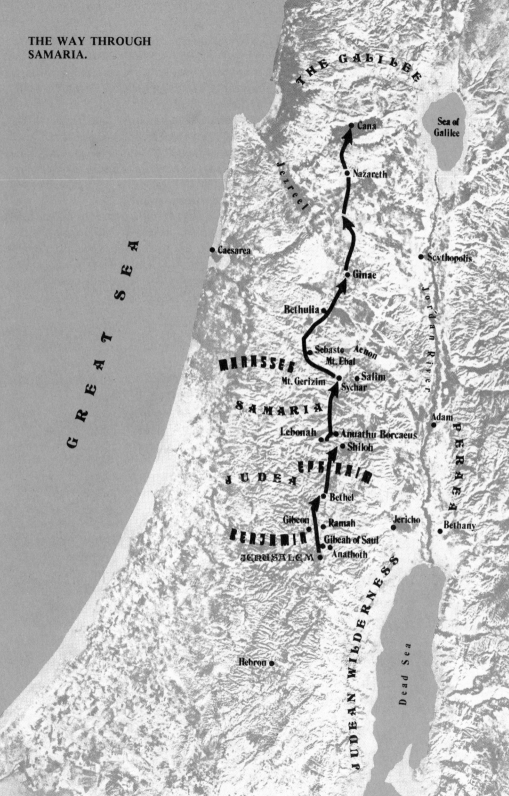

SCALE 1:1,000,000

THE WAY THROUGH
SAMARIA.

THE GALILEE

Sea of
Galilee

Cana

Nazareth

Jezreel

Caesarea

Scythopolis

Ginae

Bethulia

Jordan River

Sebaste   Aenon
          Mt. Ebal

MANASSEH

Mt. Gerizim   Salim
              Sychar

GREAT SEA

SAMARIA

PERAEA

Lebonah   Amathu Borcaeus
             Shiloh

Adam

JUDEA   EPHRAIM

Bethel

BENJAMIN

Gibeon   Ramah   Jericho
         Gibeah of Saul   Bethany
JERUSALEM   Anathoth

JUDEAN WILDERNESS

Hebron

Dead Sea

now a Samaritan shrine. It lies at the southern edge of the ruins of Shechem across a small field from Jacob's well. Judeans console themselves with the thought that the body of Joseph is not actually here, but rather has been brought to its proper resting place with the other Patriarchs in Judean Hebron. They refer to the area this May morning as Joseph's field.

The hike through the sun-drenched plain has been long and hot. The disciples are hungry. They leave a tired Jesus resting on the side of Jacob's well and go into Sychar to buy food for lunch, since it is about noon, the sixth hour. They will eat by the well on the outskirts of the village, keeping their distance from the Samaritans. Because the main source of water is in the village, they will not be bothered by crowds coming here to draw water.

No sooner have they left than a woman carrying a water jar on her head arrives to draw water from the well. How odd this is! Why does she come this extra distance to go through the laborious task of drawing water from a well instead of simply placing the jar under the spout of the accessible village spring? The ease with which she enters into a conversation with Jesus confirms any

incipient suspicion. Women do not speak so freely with strange men. Here is an example of the harlotry of which Hosea spoke. She however is doubly filthy for she is also an outcast from her own adulterous people!

The conversation does not go smoothly at first. She cannot comprehend what Jesus means when He tells her that He can give her a gift of water, although He first requested that she give Him a drink. Her thoughts are only on that deep 151-feet of well shaft into which, day after day she must lower her skin bucket time after time until her burdensome clay water jar is filled. Could He possibly provide a way that would free her from being forced to come here and draw water? Truly if He could do that He would be greater than Father Jacob. Jesus, however, is concerned with the basic reason that she has to come to this place. His next request goes to the heart of her problem. "Go, call your *husband* and come here." Her denial that she has a *husband* (baal) Jesus accepts as true. In fact, she has had five *husbands* (baalim), and the baal she now claims to have is not truly a *husband*.

JOHN 4:9-15

JOHN 4:16-19

The pass between Mounts Gerizim and Ebal — the great crossroads of the country, the true center of the Promised Land.

The talk of marriage and *husbands,* baalim, evokes thoughts of the prophet's language and naturally directs attention to the top of the mount that overshadows them. There is the holy place which Judeans claim has been

2 Kings 17:29-31 covered with temples to baalim borrowed from five pagan countries. Here the present worshipers do not truly acknowledge God as their only *husband.* She comments on His use of such language by calling Him a prophet. Her next

JOHN 4:20-24 remark acknowledges the controversy this holy place has caused. The Samaritans expect a prophet to first appear on this mount. But the Judeans claim that Jerusalem is the place where an anointed one will be manifested. Jesus does not enter into the debate. He dismisses the importance of Mount Gerizim just as He dismissed Mount Zion last month. Neither here nor Jerusalem is the true place of worship. Rather it is to be found *where He is!* Of course, He does not deny His identity. He is a Judean and the salvation which He, as a Judean, brings

JOHN 4:25-26 is thus from the Judeans. The Samaritan woman begins to understand these words. She acknowledges that the Samaritans are waiting for an anointed one. Jesus responds by proclaiming that He is that One.

When the disciples return from the village, they are shocked that Jesus is

JOHN 4:27-30 speaking with a Samaritan woman, but they make no comment. It is even more puzzling when she runs off to the village, leaving her unfilled water jar behind. She no longer needs to come here to fetch water. By that simple act, her confession of Jesus has been made. The Anointed One has revealed Himself to her and quenched her thirst. She rushes back into the society from which she has been banned and proclaims the good news to all.

The disciples are further puzzled. In spite of the arduous trek and long wait

JOHN 4:31-38 for lunch, Jesus does not immediately begin to eat. Instead, He speaks of food in terms of doing the will of the One Who sent Him. They hardly associate this

Right & upper right: Now is the time to reap what others have sown.

74

comment with the woman who has just left. Pointing to the grain fields in front of them, He continues with the saying, "four months to the harvest." It is May. Those fields were sown four months ago and now their grain-heavy stalks wave in the breeze. Now, Jesus points out, is time for the harvest. The winter planting has been carried out by John and his disciples just four miles to the north at Aenon. Now is the time for the disciples of the Anointed One to reap what others have sown.

As the Samaritans of Balluta-Sychar follow the woman to Jesus, it is clear that the harvest is already beginning. Between the hills where the first Joshua-Jesus had formed a covenant between the People and their God, a new bond is now being forged. A marriage takes place during the two days Jesus remains there.

JOHN 4:39-43

After this short sojourn, they head toward Cana, the scene of another marriage this spring. The way is not very difficult. After two hours they arrive at Sebaste, that great center of Roman domination in Samaria. As the road winds down a slight incline and around the base of the hill upon which Sebaste is built, they look up at another holy place, a pagan one. This huge temple elicits more aversion than that felt for Mount Gerizim which they have just left behind. A monumental statue to Augustus Caesar stands in the temple. It "blesses" the site of the former capital of Israel. In the east, Caesar had been given the titles of the Hellenistic conquerors before him, titles which make him a demigod. He was often called by that beloved pagan title, "savior." His huge empire and his military might, so the pagans claim, had brought "peace" to the world and made him its savior. As the disciples move past Sebaste and climb the only steep hill

Josephus,War
I, 403

separating them from the Galilee, they look back toward Mount Gerizim in the distance, marking the place of victory for them. The last acclamation of the Samaritans buoys them on their way. They who know Sebaste's domination of their land only too well have hailed not Caesar, but Jesus, as truly "the Savior of the World." Jesus has replaced not only the Judean and Samaritan holy places in the land, Mount Zion and Mount Gerizim, but that of the Roman emperor as well!

JOHN 4:42

After reaching the summit, they can see the hills of the Galilee in the distance. They now hurry to that welcoming region. They soon pass by the plain in front of the hilltop village of Sanur which was named Bethulia in that fictitious Judean book, Judith. Here is a city that became a symbol of Judean victory over the pagan forces and indirectly, because of its setting, over the Samaritans as well. Such a victory over both pagan and Samaritan now seems a reality in Jesus. Two hours later they pass through Ginae, *Garden*. Then they cross the great garden and wheat Plain of Jezreel, which this May, even more than ever, seems to reflect its name, *God Sows*. Today the words of the prophet ring true for through the work of the Baptist, *God has sown* Samaritan and Galilean for Himself in the land. Through the presence of Jesus He has betrothed them to Himself. They who were not His People have become His People. The baalim are no more and God is now their *Husband*. Yet, as they climb the hills leading into the lower Galilee, there is the unsettling thought that it is the Samaritans and the

Judith 7:1

Hosea 2:19-23

JOHN 4:44-45

The plain in front of the hilltop village of Sanur.

Galileans — those who have mixed with a pagan world — who welcome their Rabbi. This Judean (Whose family moved to the Galilee) had returned faithfully to Judah, the tribe of His ancestors, to celebrate the Passover. *But He found no honor there in His own homeland!*

A monumental statue to Augustus Caesar stands in the temple.

chapter five

Two Kinds of Healing

Capernaum is more than an innocent fishing village. It provides Herod Antipas a control center for those leaving or entering the territory of his tetrarchy, the Galilee. Merchandise going in or out of this territory can be checked and taxed on the highway running behind the village to the upper Jordan River, the eastern boundary of the Galilee. Herod maintains this control through his official representatives. These obtrusive royal officials are detested by nearly everyone in this fishing village, who await the day when Rome's heavy hand will be removed. Following Herod's lead, they have surrendered the land to Roman imperialism so they may enjoy the luxuries with which it seduces its "friends." In fact, many of these Herodians seem to place more faith in Rome than in the Creator of the world!

Reports of the triumphal return of Jesus to the Galilee soon reach Capernaum. Travelers passing along the key road down from the center of the Galilee to the plain of Gennesaret, around the lake to Capernaum, and on to Greater Syria and the east, spread the word. One of the officials of Herod's government listens eagerly to the reports of the signs and wonders worked by this Galilean during His recent visit to Judea. His little boy sweats and writhes with a burning fever aggravated by the sweltering summer heat made doubly harsh by the lake's oppressive humidity. He does not seem able to fight back death much longer. After trying all possible means of saving his son, the royal functionary sets out on the demanding journey up to Cana. It is reported the Wonder Worker is residing there. He clings to one last desperate hope. Perhaps there he will find life for his beloved boy.

JOHN 4:46-47-50

The official starts as soon as the predawn twilight assures safe travel along the way. Although the road around the lake and into the Valley of Arbel is traveled before the sun's rays begin to pound, the intense heat shimmering over the tropical Plain of Gennesaret slows the progress of the hurrying father. His desperation makes the way seem even longer and more difficult. By the second hour of the morning he enters the valley. The 20-minute walk through the valley is followed by a strenuous climb to the village of Arbel. The weary, thirsty traveler must stop in the village to refresh himself despite his anxiety to press on. Also, he is relieved that no harm came to him while he was in that narrow corridor dominated by those who are not friends of Caesar or Herod. They would have no pity for this anxious father. He is one of those Roman hirelings, revolutionaries consider traitors to the People of God, for he sold out to Rome!

The royal official leaves Arbel by midmorning. The Horns of Hittin rise before him. From below, they appear like the shell of a gigantic turtle whose neck extends out to a lower hillock which forms its head. The way to Cana winds around it. Along this turtle's side, signs of summer abound. Once-green fields are

Left:
Capernaum in the
predawn twilight

79

burnt and dry. Flies and fleas swarm about the traveler, attacking his sweating body. The dust has taken over the pathway and mixes with perspiration to form a grimy film over the exposed parts of his body. It fills his mouth with a dull, chalky taste. Having passed the third hour of its climb across the heavens, the sun burns relentlessly as the harassed Herodian turns up the steep slope behind Kefar Hittaia leading around the turtle's head. The path is almost blocked by a wall of high thistles on each side of the trail. Their thorny leaves and broken branches litter the path. When brushed by the hurrying father, they work their way into his sandals and tear at the flesh of an exposed foot, or catch the light, flowing summer dress and rip its fringes.

The once pleasant grain fields above the Horns have disappeared. Instead of the high stand of barley and wheat, the traveler is greeted by stubs of still unplowed stems left over from last month's harvest. Dust clouds picked up in the late morning breeze carry away the remaining light chaff piled about the fields on either side of the way. Despite its lifeless appearance, the way is now less taxing and eases the official's sore, tired legs as he moves along under Mount Turan, which separates him from the rich Asochis Plain and Cana. After rounding the narrow end of this long hill, he reaches Rimmon. Its pomegranate trees are now decorated with green miniatures of the large red fruit which will weigh down their branches in the fall. His sight and thoughts are directed from here to Cana, less than an hour's walk across the recently harvested Plain of Asochis.

The last leg of the journey seems the most cruel as the noon sun of the sixth hour bakes the plain. As the hill on which Cana sits is approached, a steep slope of barren rocks confronts him, with the tops of houses barely visible. There is plenty of traffic going his way as farmers return home for a midday meal and rest. The path along the south side of the hill which brings the official into the village is crowded. It is time for lunch, the seventh hour. Although weary, hungry, and thirsty, the desperate father does not pause but quickly finds Jesus.

The One Whom he approaches has performed many signs and wonders in the past months in Judea and Jerusalem. This recalls the prophet Moses, who performed signs and wonders before Pharaoh. Was not one like Moses to arise who would perform the signs and wonders of God — even before royal officials? This royal official had heard how Jesus turned water into wine when He returned here from Judea last spring. However, His sign was not like that of Moses who turned all the water of Egypt, even that in stone jars, into blood as a warning of a curse to come. *Rather Jesus gave a sign of hope and blessing for the People,* as stone water jars overflowed with the finest of wine. This was only the beginning of many blessed signs and wonders!

Jesus seems to sense the thoughts of this royal official who, like Pharaoh, represents the oppressive power in the land which has enslaved many of God's People. He accuses the royal visitor of coming to Him only because of the signs and wonders. His impatience increased by his weariness, the distraught father brushes aside Jesus' time-wasting protestations and pleads for his dying child. If He will only come down to Capernaum, his boy will be healed. Jesus gives no indication of being willing or needing to interrupt His sojourn in Cana to see the child. There is no need for this for His presence *is already there!* He tells the man to return home. His son will not die.

Ex. 7:3-4

Deut. 18:18

Ex. 7:14-19

JOHN 4:50

Left:
The narrow corridor of the Valley of Arbel above which rise the Horns of Hittin.

81

After such a tiring journey to a village so far from his home, one would expect an outburst of indignation that Jesus would not come to help. At the very least, the anxious father might turn away in silent bitterness, dejection, and utter defeat in his race for the life of his boy. There is none of that! This royal official lives close to the all-pervasive pagan world with its seductive symbols of healing and power. In spite of that, he perceives in the One before him a healing power that brings true life unhindered by distance, earthly ways, summer heat, and threatening death. He simply *trusts* Jesus. In that faith he departs for home.

After a refreshing midday meal, he begins the journey back down to Capernaum. The joy of knowing all is well further revives him. The worst of the heat is past as he crosses the Asochis Plain. A shadow lengthens at the base of Mount Turan, making the way cooler. One always seems to catch a second wind during summer afternoons! The land suddenly does not seem so lifeless. The green of trees and vines on the hillsides is highlighted by the declining sun. This gives a further feeling of new life and hope. As the hillside leading to the Horns of Hittin and the lake below is reached, Syria and the Decapolis are revealed, with Mount Hermon faintly visible far to the north. Mount Hermon is a spectacular sight in early summer and quite refreshing. Its slowly melting snow will provide strong rushing springs of life-giving water for the Galilee during September and October the driest months of the year.

JOHN 4:51-54 As the day draws to a close and the evening of the new day begins, the official reaches the broad top of Mount Arbel. In the distance, rushing toward him, he can make out the familiar faces of his house servants. Skipping the usual greetings they shout the good news. *Your son will live!* They had been dispatched after it was clear that the boy would recover. The fever had suddenly broken; his struggle with threatening death quickly ended. When the master asks the time this sudden change in the boy's condition took place, they reply that it was yesterday (that is, the beginning of the afternoon just past), at the seventh hour. Seven, that perfect number, was indeed the perfect hour!

The official continues home a new person. He now knows that the Prophet he met brings a peace and healing greater than that of any of the Romans to whom he had bowed. His family now begins to follow a Savior of the world who is far greater than Caesar. He is greater than any of the healing gods of the pagans to whom he had previously turned in desperation to save his son. This One, without magic, special ritual, or even touching — simply by a Word — brings life from death!

JOHN 5:1 After spending the summer in the Galilee, Jesus and His disciples return again to Jerusalem for *the* festival of the year, Succoth. It is the beginning of October when they leave the Galilee by way of the Jezreel. The soil on the hillsides is a bright rust-red, speckled here and there with bleached stubble, a remnant of the grain harvests long past. This contrasts to the rich greenness of the valley floor. Life-giving springs still pour from the base of Mount Gilboa in this driest of months and are a sign of the Feast of Succoth about to begin in Deut. 16:16-17 Jerusalem. This is one of the three major festivals which all males of the People of God should attend annually. It is often especially designated as *the* festival.

The purpose of Succoth is prayer for rain during the coming winter months so the springs will continue to flow and the dry hillsides will once again flourish.

SCALE 1:1,000,000

**THE WAY TO THE FEAST
OF SUCCOTH IN JERUSALEM.**

THE GALILEE

Capernaum

Gennesaret

Sea of
Galilee

Cana

Rimmon • Mt. Turan

Gadara

Sepphoris

Nazareth

DECAPOLIS

Jezreel

Harod •

Mt. Gilboa

Scythopolis

Pella

GREAT SEA

Jordan River

Jabbok River

SAMARIA

PERAEA

Arimathea

JUDEA

Jericho

Bethany

JERUSALEM • Bethany

JUDEAN WILDERNESS

Dead Sea

As they pass small ponds fed by springs such as Harod, they catch glimpses of that elusive creature, the snake. The Galilee is also a serpent's paradise. This creature draws admiration because of its shrewd knowledge of the land. It knows exactly how to save the creation from pests such as mice that would destroy it. The snake also knows exactly where to get food, even in the desert areas of the south. It survives by its skill at quickly catching its prey. The temptation to *Gen. 3:1* idolize it is indeed strong. Eve was not the only one ensnared by this cunning

beast. Passing by the temple of Asclepius, the god of healing, in Scythopolis, one is reminded that people still bow to this creature in the hope of escape from dreaded death and pain. The pagans claim the snake is Asclepius' messenger. Dionysus, the god of the vine, may be the most popular of the pagan gods among the common folk, holding out the hope of life after death, but Asclepius runs a close second, because Asclepius can forestall death!

They leave the Galilee by way of Jezreel.

An idolatrous
people honors
Asclepius as the
true bringer of life.

One swift strike of
the carpet viper's
head spells instant
death.

The story of this revered healer (usually depicted lifting up a staff around which a snake is entwined) is typical of the confused tales of these pagans. Rather than a good creation brought forth from the Word of the Creator, they know only a universe where gods battle other gods and human beings. The mother of Asclepius, so they explain, made the fatal mistake of trying to be the lover of both a god and a mortal. The god Apollo was enraged when he discovered her infidelity and struck her dead. Apollo was immediately sorry for his rash action. As her body was being cremated, he saved the child she was carrying in her womb. This was his child, of course. He was named Asclepius. A centaur, half-man and half-horse, brought him up and taught him all knowledge of medicine. He finally became so advanced in the art of healing that (so pagans claim) he raised the dead! The supreme pagan deity, Zeus, was outraged that a mortal should have power over death and killed Asclepius with one of his thunderbolts.

Nevertheless, an idolatrous world now honors Asclepius as the bringer of life. Temples are erected to him such as this one at Scythopolis. The serpent plays an important part in the ritual observed in these shrines. It brings the healing power of this son of Apollo to the pagans who look to it with the hope of escaping sickness and death.

Gen. 3:1-20 The desolate Jordan Valley, hazy and shimmering in the early October heat, impresses upon the traveler the result of placing trust in that reptile. Arid dust swirls up from fields that must be worked by the sweat of the brow to ease hunger. Thorns cover the hillsides and sneak into the fields to choke the crops. Not the life promised by the snake, but death came to mortals who now return to the fine dust which is blown away before Jesus' followers — the stuff from which they were created. The hope expressed at the Feast of Succoth is for the termination of that curse of the serpent-induced expulsion from Eden. The People hope for a final day of joy when paradise will return from which they will not be cast out and in which they will no longer know sickness or death.

After they cross the Jordan River near Bethany of Peraea and head up the desert way to Jerusalem, the disciples are a bit more careful of where they step. A deadly carpet viper darts across their path, in no way encumbered by its cursed leglessness. They are reminded that the serpent is not only a symbol for healing — one swift strike of its diamond-shaped head spells instant death.

As they look south across the Dead Sea, they recall that in the days of the Exodus venomous serpents attacked the followers of Moses. God used this pagan symbol of healing to save a repentant wilderness generation whose sin had led to serpent-inflicted death. Anyone who would look to the snake would be healed. As they continue their climb to Jerusalem, the words of Jesus to Nicodemus in that city last Passover reecho. Jesus seemed to equate Himself with the pagan symbol God had used so that death might pass over the people after they sinned in the wilderness. Cryptically, He claimed that even as Moses lifted up that healing serpent, so must He too be lifted up. Those who looked to Him and trusted in Him at that *lifting up* would receive true salvation. This life would not be for the fleeting moment of such as those healed in the desert or in a shrine to Asclepius might know, but forever. He is greater than any wilderness serpent.

Later, during one of their visits to the Temple during the Feast of Succoth, the feast of prayer for life, Jesus goes outside the city, just north of the Holy Place, to the district of Bethzatha. A gate through which sheep are brought to the Temple area for sacrifice leads to this district which lies in the shadow of the Antonia fortress. Roman soldiers and their dependents are much in evidence as they congregate around their secure fortress thrust in the side of God's Holy Place. In addition to the Romans coming and going on patrol, there is much civilian traffic along this way north of the city. Farmers go out to their fields and merchants head toward the Jericho Road. Here one feels the clash of worlds in Jerusalem: east and west, Greek and Hebrew, occupier and occupied, farmer and merchant, pagan and God's People. One senses their incompatibility as well.

A deep, but short valley runs diagonally through this district and adds protection to the northern end of the Temple area as it enters into the Kidron Valley. A dam built across the valley forms the middle of two huge reservoirs which collect the precious rainwater falling in this area. This provides another water supply area for Jerusalem. Herod the Great and his predecessors, the Hasmonians, had built such reservoirs around Jerusalem to provide water for the ever-expanding city. The same technique for turning a valley into a reservoir had even been utilized far away from the city, south of Bethlehem. This vital water was then brought to Jerusalem by aqueduct. Because of the size of this city by the edge of the desert, it cannot solely depend on the living waters of the Gihon Spring feeding the Pool of Siloam. The still water of the cisterns under its buildings and its reservoirs, like Bethzatha's, are all-important. During this week-long Feast of Succoth, all of God's People who are gathered in Jerusalem will

Numbers 21:4-9

John 3:14-15

Josephus,War V, 149-151

John 5: 1-9

p 87f

The same
technique for
turning a valley
into a reservoir
had been used
south of
Bethlehem.

pray for rain to fill reservoirs like this one whose water supply is nearly depleted. When full, the two basins formed by the dammed valley can hold enough water in their 44-foot depth to meet the demand of this northern suburb of the city. The Antonia and Temple area also draw water from it. Because sheep are washed in this area before being taken to the Temple for sacrifice, the reservoir is called the Sheep Pool.

JOHN 5:2-3

As Jesus approaches the Sheep Pool, His attention is not drawn to the great basins, but rather to the five porches arranged in the form of a pentagon beside them. People turn from the way to join the crowd gathered about this complex. As the disciples join them, it is obvious that the gathering is anything but normal. In front of them a man hobbles along on a crutch. Several others carry a girl who seems to be on the threshold of death. There is another who clutches a marble foot in his hand as he walks gingerly on a newly healed foot. He places the piece of marble, inscribed in Greek, at the center of the porches as if it were an offering! What particularly catches the eye, however, is a finely carved marble plaque carried by one of the Romans. He talks excitedly with his companions, nodding to the porches and gesturing with delight to the object on the plaque which he lifts up for all to see. A coiled serpent with human head stares back at its admirers from the marble. This is Serapis, another form of Asclepius, which belongs to eastern tradition where the healing god is the snake itself. In the Holy Land, the pagan world of east and west meet and mingle. One understands, even without knowing Latin, that this man is expressing thanksgiving and joyous satisfaction. He knows the name of this healer well, as one hears him repeat it over and over again.

88

Far left:
A marble foot inscribed in Greek.

Serapis, a form of Asclepius belonging to Eastern tradition.

This place is well-known although it is despised by the leaders in God's beautiful House which rises in majesty behind it. In the Holy City, not only do pagan imperialists keep God's Sanctuary under control with the bullying bulk of the Antonia, but they also support the shrine of the god of healing and life. This is Asclepius or Serapis, whose temple in pagan Scythopolis had been passed with such disgust a few days ago. If Jerusalem is thought to retain a remnant of paradise lost, and holds out the promise of being the center of a returned paradise when life-giving water will stream from the altar rock at the final Succoth, then that cunning beast of the garden is still not far away. It continues to beguile, bewitch and offer false hopes of healing and victory over death. Unfortunately, the presence of the healing snake is nothing new to the Holy City. After all, that bronze serpent of the desert, which God had used as His instrument to heal the lost among the followers of Moses, had been turned into an idol and brought to Jerusalem. They had burned incense to it at the place of God's footstool until Hezekiah finally smashed it to pieces. Now the serpent has been restored north of the Temple in the shrine Jesus enters.

2 Kings 18:1-4

Patients lie waiting for help in the porches which protect them from the declining, but still hot sun of early October. Obviously, pagans are not the only visitors to the shrine. God's People are also present. Perhaps they have excused themselves from God's care for a moment when their prayers for healing seemed to go unanswered, and have come here out of desperation to find the healing spirit. It is easy enough to rationalize away the contradiction this represents to the faith in the one true God. They might argue that this is another way God works; it is just a slightly different form. Did not God heal the wilderness generation with the serpent? People *do* claim to go away cured, so what can be wrong with this?

Near the porches are several shallow immersion pools with a few steps leading into them. They are filled with patients bathing themselves. Other patients can be seen smearing mud on their afflicted parts. They perform prescribed rituals of walking and running about the area, followed by a bath and massage. There are also small grottoes where patients may bathe in soothing water as they rest in the semidarkness. In some grottoes the sick sleep, hoping that in their dreams the healing spirit or its messenger, the snake, might reveal a cure.

Small grottoes where patients may bathe in the semidarkness.

JOHN 5:5-9

Jesus turns to one of the patients lying beside an immersion pool and asks if he wants to be healed. Rather than answer what would seem to be the most important question for him, he is too preoccupied with the superstition connected with this pool. He points to the water and those grouped around it and begins to complain. Every time the healing spirit comes and ripples the water by the breeze (a sign of the spirit's presence), he is unable to get down the few steps leading into the water fast enough to be the one who receives the gift of healing. He is desperate, for he has been sick 38 years. Nobody will help him beat the crowd, he complains, by throwing him into the pool.

Jesus, ignoring the cripple's addiction to such superstition, orders him to get up, take his bed, and walk. Instantly he is healed, although he has not asked Jesus for healing. Feeling the movement coming back into his legs, he stands as Jesus is almost inundated by the crowd of patients pushing and shoving to get near the pools or grottoes as they seek instant cure. He is carried away by the flow of the crowd. The healed cripple, meanwhile, unlike the official in the Galilee *who responded to Jesus in faith* without even seeing that healing had taken place, picks up his mattress and starts out from the shrine.

As he passes through Bethzatha, he is stopped by indignant Pharisees who JOHN 5:9-13 inform him that by doing such work as carrying a mattress he is breaking the Sabbath. Has he no respect for the laws of Moses? Rather than accept responsibility for his action, he who has just been freed from such a shrine, tries

to push the blame onto the One Who has cured him. When they inquire as to His name, he cannot answer. Incredible as it might seem, although he had been suffering for so long, he had not attempted to find Jesus in the crowd, or at least learn the name of his benefactor.

Shallow immersion pools with a few steps leading into them.

Later, when he does not come to Him, Jesus must seek out this healed cripple. He finds him in the Temple area just across from the shrine. How unresponsive is this former cripple! Instead of receiving immediate heartfelt thanks for healing him, Jesus must remind him that he is now better. Jesus does not indulge this ungrateful one. He warns him to sin no more and to avoid that place where he had grasped for straw hopes. False healing will only lead to death. Faith must not be placed in superstitious cures which in the end are not cures at all. In God alone must one's faith rest when things do not seem to go as well as they should. He must never go that way again, Jesus warns, so that nothing worse than sickness will come to him.

JOHN 5:14

Jesus' warning falls on deaf ears, for the man is blind to the faith to which Jesus is pointing. He does not show even a small gesture of gratitude! Unlike the official returning to his loved ones and spreading the good news of faith in the Healer, he troops off to the Pharisees to report that the One Who forced him to violate the Sabbath and Whose name he could not produce at the time, is called Jesus! His report causes the opposition to Jesus to grow stronger among some Judeans who seem more worried about the technical points of the Mosaic law

JOHN 5:15-24

than about the crippled soul of the man before them. When they confront Jesus at this feast of life, challenging His healing on a Sabbath, He explains that the healing took place because of His Father Who is working in Him. An inevitable collision course seems to impend. They will seek to kill this blasphemer Who would dare to make Himself equal with God.

Pointing in the direction of the shrine to the north of the city where many a JOHN 5:25-47 wayward member of the People of God have sought escape from death, Jesus proclaims that the *dead will find life only in Him*. The listeners' attention is also drawn to the hills about Jerusalem which are dotted with tombs and funerary monuments. Some of these tombs go back to the time of David, others are still

being prepared such as that of the family of a Joseph from Arimathea located just outside the city wall on the northwest. One realizes that Jerusalem is actually the center of a graveyard. Who among those standing on the Temple Mount and looking out on the surrounding hills does not also have thoughts of his own inevitable death?

Standing in the middle of this cemetery, Jesus proclaims that an hour is coming when all who are in these graves will hear His voice. They will come forth to Life if they have kept themselves free from the pagan and secular forces surrounding them. If they put their faith in creatures like the serpent, or power structures of the world like Caesar's, they will be judged accordingly. Now is the beginning of the judgment which determines death or Life!

The hills about Jerusalem are dotted with tombs and funerary monuments.

Ancient Mound

chapter six

The Manna Descends

*And those who have hungered shall rejoice,
moreover, also they shall behold marvels
everyday. For winds shall go forth from
before Me to bring every morning the
fragrance of aromatic fruits, and at the
close of the day clouds distilling
the dew of health. And it shall come to pass
at the selfsame time that the treasury of
manna shall again descend from on high,
and they will eat of it in those years,
because these are they who have come to
the consummation of time. And it shall
come to pass after these things, when the
time of the advent of the Anointed One is
fulfilled, that He shall return in glory.*

2 Baruch 29:6-30:1

Such are the hopes of the disciples as they return to the Galilee with Jesus after spending the winter in Jerusalem and Judea.

Their destination, the northern part of the Sea of Galilee, is reached by descending to the Jordan Valley, hiking its length to the south shore of the lake, and then taking a boat to the other side for the last part of the journey.

JOHN 6:1

Rather than crossing the Jordan River at Jericho, they opt to travel through the Jericho Plain on the first part of their journey to the north. The long hours on this monotonously flat way give time for reflection. Thoughts at this time of year, which is shortly before the second Passover season the disciples will spend with Jesus, naturally focus on the Exodus. After all, that decisive event in the formation of the People of God ended just across from the city through which they now pass. Soon after leaving Jericho and the ancient mound believed to be the site where Joshua fought the battle marking the beginning of the conquest, they head toward the former site of Gilgal. After a twenty-minute walk they pass near it. Except for a few houses that mark this once-important cult center, Gilgal is deserted.

How easy it is to picture Joshua entering the Promised Land. The leaders came first, carrying the twelve stones on their shoulders, trailed by a grand procession of the congregation following the ark of the covenant. They entered through the chalk hills of the inner Jordan Valley passing through the flat, gently sloping barren fields leading to this first encampment in the Promised Land.

Left:
The disciples
travel through the
Jericho Plain.

Josh. 3-4

95

Their arrival at Gilgal was marked by the disappearance of the manna which was a symbol of the Exodus. This bread from heaven had sustained a murmuring People who feared death in the wilderness. After gathering it, they formed it into cakes similar to the small, round barley loaves eaten today. They always ate until they were full despite their murmuring. This bread from heaven ceased two weeks after the establishment of their encampment at Gilgal. This marked the first Passover in their new homeland. The land would now provide them with their daily bread. The cessation of the manna took place at the time of the barley harvest in the Jericho Plain, even as today the fields of grain are ready for the sickle. The unleavened barley bread eaten during the first Passover in the Promised Land served as a reminder of the haste with which God's People departed Egypt, having no time for the proper preparation of dough. It was also a sign that the Exodus was ended.

Josh. 5:10-12

Ex. 16:2-21

Num 11:7-9

To be sure, this Promised Land was no paradise. Conquest was first required to secure farm land. Then much toil followed to make the land continue to flow with milk and honey. As they move out of the southern part of the Jericho Plain and through the desert separating it from Archelaus, the next oasis, one might even wonder if the People really escaped the wilderness. The barren hills rising on the left, chalky soil underfoot, and the bleached-out appearance of the landscape in the harsh noon sun, give the land an unrelenting drabness. Archelaus, situated near a spring, breaks the monotony and provides welcome relief as its rows of palm trees shade the travelers from the blazing sun.

Just past this oasis town at Migdal, *Tower,* the challenge of this land is easily observed. Workers blackened by the sun struggle to clear the wasteland of its only natural vegetation, the cursed thorns. They also labor to bring life-giving water into this desolate land by constructing and repairing a series of criss-crossing irrigation aqueducts and ditches. Some of these water carriers come from as far as the spring of Ephraim, seven miles away. Even in this scorching heat an army of human ants persists in its battle with the soil, plowing and fertilizing.

Another theme of Passover is brought to mind with this sight. In the synagogues during this time before Passover, the Scripture readings assigned as preparation for the feast tell of Adam driven out of paradise and forced to make the land produce. Before the disciples lies the consequence of Adam's foolish eating of the fruit that meant his death even as he strove to gain life. As outcasts from paradise, people must struggle even in the Promised Land to provide bread that will but momentarily forestall inevitable death. This Passover, everyone longs for the return of a manna that will end the death of the present desert existence and lead the way to a true paradise of everlasting life. That hope is well symbolized in the tree the workers strive to strengthen so that it will bear rich fruit. The green palm of the desert is a symbol of life for a waiting People.

Gen. 3:3, 17-24

As the day draws to a close, they enter the northernmost part of the Jericho Plain whose center is the city of Phasaelis. It is named after the beloved brother of Herod the Great who was a casualty of the Herodian family's bid for power. Careful use of springs in the nearby hillsides has turned this desert floor into a green and welcome resting place for weary travelers. From the slight rise in the terrain, Jesus and His disciples look out over a sea of dark green palms broken

Josephus,War I, 418

Left:
The green palm of the desert is a symbol of life for a waiting people.

by chartreuse waves of newly-sprouted branches. Here and there the rows of well-groomed trees are interrupted by patches of perfume-producing balsam, appearing like thick, black-green thorn bushes. That much wealth surrounds Phasaelis becomes evident as the travelers emerge from under the rows of palms to enter the finely-built town. About Phasaelis lie beautiful plantation houses where wealthy Herodians live in pampered ease.

As the sunlight disappears over the hills of Samaria, its last rays highlight the hills to the north. These form the end of the Jericho Plain. The almost inaccessible highest peak provides a perfect lookout and control post, not only for the rich Plain of Jericho, but also for the entry valley to Samaria on its north. As would be expected, the palatial buildings adorning it form yet another Herodian stronghold, the Alexandrium. This guard post is the counterpart to Cyprus at the southern end of the plain. Its presence serves to underscore that even the splendor of a man-made paradise in the Jericho Plain is not a place for true, worry-free relaxation or assured, enduring wealth.

Early next morning, Jesus and His followers pass by the mount topped by the sentinel of the Alexandrium and move eastward in order to cross the Jordan River. After an hour's walk, they arrive at the ancient crossing point at Adam which is still another reminder of the Exodus. Here the Jordan River was blocked so that the first Joshua-Jesus could enter the Promised Land on a dry riverbed.

Josh. 3:16

The mount topped by the sentinel of the Alexandrium.

Alexandrium

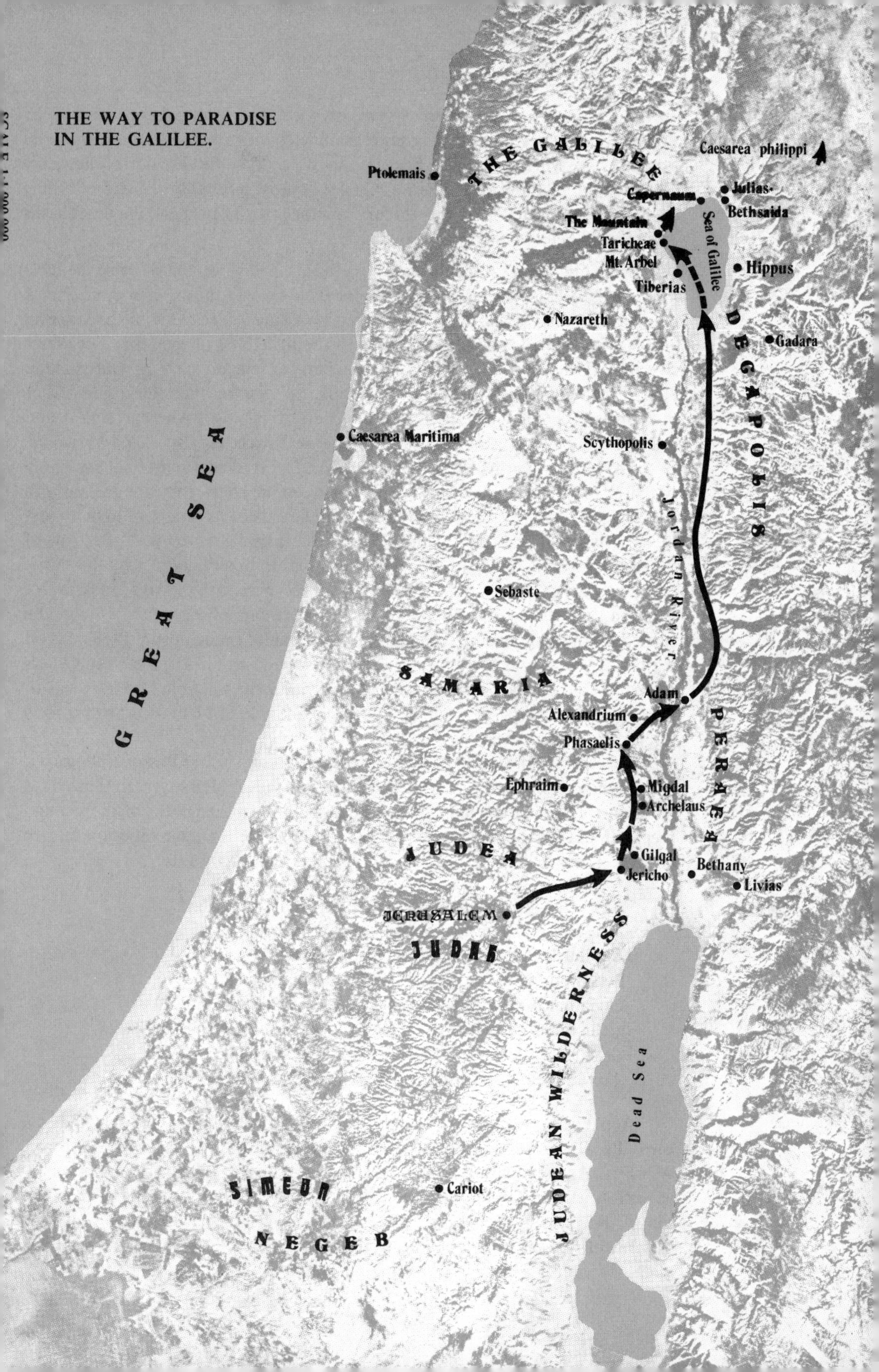

THE WAY TO PARADISE
IN THE GALILEE.

GREAT SEA

THE GALILEE

Ptolemais

Caesarea philippi

Capernaum   Julias
Bethsaida
The Mountain
Taricheae   Sea of Galilee
Mt. Arbel
Tiberias   Hippus

Nazareth   Gadara

DECAPOLIS

Caesarea Maritima

Scythopolis

Jordan River

PERAEA

Sebaste

SAMARIA

Adam

Alexandrium
Phasaelis

Ephraim
Migdal
Archelaus

JUDEA
Gilgal   Bethany
Jericho   Livias

JERUSALEM

JUDAS

JUDEAN WILDERNESS

SIMEON
Cariot

Dead Sea

NEGEB

In this pre-Passover season the river is swollen. The fording is not easy. They cross here not only to avoid any unpleasant encounters with Samaritans who do not know the Master, but also because the route along the east side of the valley to the southern shore of the Sea of Galilee is most direct. By the end of a long second day's journey, they are not far from the lake. They spend the night in the territory of Gadara of the Decapolis.

By midmorning on the third day, they are standing on the shore of the lake. The lower Jordan River is not in sight for it enters into the valley a quarter of a mile up the western shore. The unbroken shoreline is decked with thick spring grass which provides a perfect border to the light blue of the lake. The water sweeps out in front of them, with the familiar places such as Capernaum, Heptapegon, and Bethsaida barely visible specks on the other side. After boarding a boat they set sail in the direction of Tiberias. After passing it and skirting Mount Arbel, they prepare to land at Taricheae, also called Magdala.

The harbor is crowded with dinghies and larger, deepwater boats unloading the catch of the past night. Making way between the boats, they are greeted with the cries of fishermen they know well. Taricheae is at its height of activity just before Passover. The city's name, *Dried Fish,* is explained by row after row of salted fish hanging to dry in the warm April sun. In other buildings by the shore, fish are being packed carefully in brine, spiced with just the right measure of herbs to satisfy the most discriminating palates. Jars of these fish will soon be carried up the way leading through the lower Galilee to the port of Ptolemais on the Great Sea. From there they will be transported by ship to the west. Others will be packed on wagons to be carried to Syria. Some will even find their way to the great desert outposts in the east. How odd to think of fish as providing food for people in the desert!

This fish for the world being prepared in the days before Passover, however, is as nothing compared to the great banquet at the last Passover. In those days the monster fish, Leviathan, will be dragged up from the depths of the sea and prepared, not for the rich and powerful, but rather for the remnant of the People of God. How well those longing for that day can picture it:

2 Baruch 29:2-4

And it shall come to pass; when all is accomplished
that was to come to pass in those parts, that the
Anointed One shall then begin to be revealed. And
Behemoth shall be revealed from his place and
Leviathan shall ascend from the sea... those two
great monsters which I created on the fifth day of
Creation and shall have kept until that time and
then they shall be for food for all that are left.

As Jesus moves through the narrow streets of Taricheae, He is greeted as a hero. People crowd merely to get a glimpse of this Worker of Signs and Wonders. As they leave the town behind, the beauty of spring seems to support hopes for new life. On the left, the steep side of Mount Arbel sweeps up from the end of the Plain of Gennesaret like a green velvet drapery studded with crazy patterns of flowers in a rainbow of colors. It appears to be hanging suspended

Five small loaves
of coarse barley
bread and two
small fishes.

from the sheer, cave-pocked, grey rock wall rising to Arbel's summit. The stark contrast of rock and life heightens the beauty of the hill's stony crown. The flat field below is now spongy thick with grass upon which cows graze, as well as some lambs who are being fattened in one last moment of luxurious pleasure before their slaughter at the coming Passover.

Behind the plain rises a dominating mount. Its lower slope gently rises toward an isolated hump-like peak. Jesus climbs this lower slope and sits with His disciples. From here they can take in a magnificent view of the lake. It is evidently a favorite place for instruction. The mount, however, is not isolated but overlooks the traffic coming and going through the Valley of Arbel. Indeed, its central location, dominant position, and splendid panorama make it *the* mount for the disciples and Jesus.

JOHN 6:2-14

The mount is in no way a retreat center during this pre-Passover in the Galilee. The Rabbi is too well-known and has attracted too great a following. The majority of the crowd gathering below is made up of those who have followed Him from Taricheae. It is supplemented with the curious from surrounding villages who have quickly responded to reports of His return. Others on their way along the main road running between the mount and Mount Arbel join the swelling crowd.

Jesus does not turn away from the hundreds gathering below Him as lunch time approaches. He asks Philip, who knows the area well, having done much business at Taricheae, how they can possibly provide lunch for such a multitude. There is no problem, of course, in getting the food. Places where bread can be purchased are within easy walking distance. All the fish one could eat are at Taricheae, a mere 20 minute round trip from the mount. Money is the problem! How could they pay for the food such a crowd would consume? Philip's analysis of this situation (Jesus, of course, knows exactly what He will do) shows that he is an astute businessman. Quickly estimating the crowd at about 5,000, not counting women and children, and noting the current prices for bread and fish, he figures that it will take more than a common laborer earns in half a year to cover the cost.

Andrew, who evidently has been mingling with those waiting below, reports that there is a little boy who has brought his lunch. There is nothing extraordinary about this. His lunch basket contains the typical fare of the people working by the lake. He has five small loaves of coarse, cheap but nourishing barley bread, and two small dried fish, low-priced rejects not good enough for export. With seven pieces of such fare how could *anyone* possibly be satisfied, is Andrew's sarcastic question. He sounds like a complaining Moses in the wilderness.

Jesus asks the disciples to instruct the people to lie down on the grass. The JOHN 6:10 scene is indeed marvelous. Thousands recline as they will at the coming Passover, resting on their left sides, their right hands free to partake of the meal. Their cushions have become the soft, sweet-smelling spring grass covered with a fine cloth of daisies, straw-flowers, anemones, and dandelions. The mount in front becomes the place of honor with Jesus at the head of the festal table. All eyes are turned to Him as the crowd waits for the meal to begin with the blessing of the bread.

As the head of the family takes bread and offers a prayer of thanksgiving at JOHN 6:11-13 the beginning of the Passover meal, so Jesus takes the barley bread from the lad who has offered Him his lunch, giving thanks to His Father. He then begins to pass it around. He distributes the fish in the same manner. Like the food provided during the Exodus, the loaves and fish more than satisfy everyone's hunger. When the leftovers are collected, twelve full baskets of fragments from the barley loaves are brought back to Jesus. An awe-filled crowd immediately recognizes the work of a prophet like Moses. He feeds the People, however, not *Deut. 18:18* like Moses in the wilderness, but in the paradise of the Galilean spring. This certainly is the perfect setting for the proclamation of their prophet-king and the JOHN 6:14-15 fulfillment of their hopes. Here freedom fighters had so often found refuge from the oppressive pagan forces as they hid in the caves dotting **Mount Arbel**. Here The Mount

the throng of God's People moves, keeping its distance from Roman-dominated Tiberias. Just as they are about to rush forward and force Him to be that king, Jesus abruptly moves to the isolated peak of the mount. The disappointed crowd is left to disperse at its leisure. He will not let them have that moment of triumph they so crave, slipping away before they can hurry the future *hour* appointed for His enthronement.

JOHN 6:16-17 Late in the afternoon the disciples head back to Taricheae to sail across to Capernaum, the center of Jesus' ministry by the lake. Jesus wishes to remain alone on the mount. As evening approaches, there is much activity at the harbor. Fishermen are preparing for the night's work. Soon the fish will begin feeding on insects which seem to appear from nowhere as dusk turns to night.

JOHN 6:18 As they set sail across the lake in the direction of Capernaum, all seems perfect. However, no sooner is the shore left behind than one of those terrible winds that can appear without warning tears around the lake, whipping up high waves. Such winds are dreaded by the sailors for they have no prevailing direction, being swirled around in the bowl formed by the hills surrounding the lake. Sail is quickly replaced by oar as the disciples try to make headway in the darkness. In their wildly pitching boat, constantly being inundated with water JOHN 6:19-21 which they must frantically keep bailing out, the time it takes the terror-stricken crew to row three or four miles seems endless.

Jesus, meanwhile, leaves the mount and crosses the Plain of Gennesaret on foot. He moves much faster than the boat struggling out on the lake. The moon, growing to fullness before the Passover festival, occasionally illuminates the scene as it breaks through the low clouds. After an hour's walk, Jesus arrives at the foot of the hill upon which the ancient city of Gennesaret once stood. The boat tosses madly not far from the shore.

Although the lake is rather shallow in this area and a major docking place on the north shore is not far away, their craft is so caught by the wind and waves that the occupants are terrified for their lives. At any moment, it seems, they may be thrown into the turbulence. Jesus moves quickly along the water to the boat, Ps. 107:23-32 comforting and assuring the disciples that they need have no fear. He Who was the creating Word at the beginning, Who brought dry land from water, is by their side. Their fear vanishes and they rejoice that He is in their midst. Immediately they land on the nearby shore. They have found a harbor safe from wind, wave, and darkness. In the security of His company, they head for Capernaum only two miles away. With His presence it becomes indeed *Village* (Caper) *of Comfort* (Naum).

During the night, word of the marvelous feast spreads with the speed of the storm throughout the villages by the lake, and reaches Tiberias. The next morning JOHN 6:22-23 some people from this city go to the place where the wonder was performed with the hope of catching a repeat performance. As they climb into their small dinghies docked by Tiberias' long harbor front and prepare for the easy trip around Arbel to Taricheae, they appear a mixed lot. They suit the city which they have recently chosen for their home.

The city they leave behind is composed of a long, narrow strip of buildings in various stages of completion. Only a decade ago Herod Antipas, with Roman consent of course, decided to build this city so that he might better control the

eastern part of the Galilee. This new location also helps strengthen the defense against any attack on the empire's eastern front. The task of finding land for the capital was not easy. The only area on the west shore left undeveloped lay immediately south of Mount Arbel. Unfortunately, there was a major drawback. This is the site of an extensive graveyard. As Herod Antipas built his city on top of a resting place of the dead, the devout of God's People immediately avoided any prolonged contact with it. To enter homes in Tiberias means immediate uncleanness because of possible contact with one of the graves. Revolutionaries, of course, have as little as possible to do with a city encroaching on their domain. It was founded in part, after all, to curtail their activities. Herod is forced to try every means possible to induce the People of God to settle here. Those left without an inheritance, or recently liberated from their masters, grab at this opportunity to acquire cheap property. Also, sharp businessmen take advantage of the incentives offered for starting businesses here. This has led to the complaint that only the dregs of society make up its population. Most residents are pro-Roman and beholden to the government. The overcrowded Galilee also has many pagans who gladly accept Herod's offers. The population is varied and opportunistic. Many are of the type that is always looking for a handout, rushing like beggars to any benefactor.

After passing Tiberias and skirting Mount Arbel, they prepare to land at Taricheae.

Josephus, Antiquities XIII, 36-38

How incongruous
their murmuring
seems here. In the
desert the People
were surrounded
with nothing but
rock, dirt, and dust.

Josephus, Life, 65

JOHN 6:24

JOHN 6:25-51

Josephus, War
III, 41 44

Nevertheless, the city is certainly not poor. Herod's magnificent palace overlooking the city sets a fast pace for all the status-seekers below. Located on the top of the steep cliff rising behind the middle of the city, its white limestone facade provides a fine contrast to the black basalt homes below. It is well known that inside are fine statues of nudes and animals in marble and precious metals, fixtures of gold and silver, and fine furniture made from the best wood Lebanon or the West can provide. The mixed nature of its population is noted by the casual acceptance of Herod's enjoyment of the these statues of humans and animals so strongly prohibited by Moses. Probably not a few of these even represent the hated pagan gods of the overlord Romans who Antipas loves to imitate. Indeed, he has shamelessly proclaimed his true loyalties by calling the city Tiberias.

When the Tiberians arrive at Taricheae, they find to their disappointment that the Wonder Worker has departed. Others from this village who are anxious to see another wonder join them in sailing to Capernaum where the disciples were last reported to be heading. On a clear day, refreshed and cleansed by the storm of the past night, their boats run under full sail, giving the appearance of a flotilla moving slowly across the lake. They find the One Who is the center of their curiosity soon after landing at Capernaum.

Jesus is teaching at the synagogue in the open court of the school area next to the worship hall. He greets them with the challenge that they have come not because of His signs, but simply because some had their bellies filled with bread. As He talks of food, the bounty of the Galilee (accentuated at this time before Passover) surrounds them. Fishermen are hurrying to get their last night's catch to the processing center of Taricheae. The hills are dotted with fattening sheep.

Further up the slopes, cattle can be seen being herded from one lush pasture to another. Fruit orchards around the lake are in blossom or already supporting the green beginnings of the delicious fruits of the fall. Row after row of vegetables are ready for picking. Behind Capernaum, wagons on the main road to the east testify to the wealth of goods pouring out of the Galilee and to the luxuries being imported. Those living around the lake willingly put in long hours of hard labor to be able to purchase these fine luxuries.

The bounties of the Galilee surround them.

Jesus, however, begins to speak about food that does not perish in contrast to that with which they strive to fill their warehouses. Rather than this ephemeral wealth and satisfaction, He pleads with those about Him to labor for food which will never perish! This is food that is even better than that manna which their ancestors ate during their first two weeks in the Promised Land. That manna, like the present riches of the Galilee's fields and lake, quickly disappeared.

Jesus' audience replies that they want a clearer sign that they will receive something better for their toil, although such an extraordinary sign seems impossible in the spring of the Galilee. They need such a sign for belief in Him, a tangible sign such as Moses provided with the manna. After clarifying that it was not Moses but His Father Who gave the manna, Jesus proclaims that God now gives the true Bread, the *new* Manna. They excitedly beg for this. His further explanation seems odd, however. *He* claims to be that Bread of Life. He is the One Who is greater than the fruits of field or lake. He declares that those who believe in Him will truly reenter the paradise from which their ancestors were cast out and left to labor and sweat, whether that be on the barren hills of Judea, or the rich plains about Gennesaret. To all who come to Him, *He will give the Food of Eternal Life!*

Gen. 3:24

JOHN 6:52-65

A number of Judeans who are in Capernaum on business and have come to listen to this well-known Wonder Worker, murmur at His comments. They murmur like the congregation of Moses in the desolate wilderness of the south.

Ex. 16:4-12

Yet, how incongruous their murmuring seems here! In the desert the People were surrounded with nothing but rock, dirt, and dust combined with the nagging boredom of eating manna day after day. There the People faced the constant threat of starvation and thirst. Here within this fruitful land stands One Who not only fed them well, but offers the way to eternal life. Yet, they murmur! As the wilderness generation reacted to perishable manna, so they murmur at the new and perfect Manna Who offers Himself to them. Unlike Nathanael a year ago in Bethany of Peraea, they can see nothing special about this One. He is simply the son of Joseph and Mary from the humble town of Nazareth.

Jesus does not retreat in the face of their adverse reaction, but presses His claims even further. Unlike Adam who ate the forbidden fruit and died, those who partake of Him will never die. Although His audience begins to drift away at such talk, He unrelentingly persists in His demand that, in order to pass from death to true life, *they eat of His flesh and drink of His blood!* The thinning circle

Lev. 17:10

gathered about Him in the court of the Capernaum synagogue is horrified and shocked. Had not Moses forbidden the eating of an animal's blood — then how much more strongly, human blood? To them, the thought of eating human flesh and drinking human blood is repulsive, something a mystic rite of the pagans who face the Galilee in the Decapolis might demand. Blood is not consumed, because blood is reserved for sacrifice at the altar in Jerusalem. The blood of the lamb, instead of the human sacrifices of the barbaric pagans, is what atones for the People. Moses made this clear:

Lev. 17:11

> For the life of the flesh is in the blood;
> and I have given it for you upon the
> altar to make atonement for your souls;
> for it is the blood that makes
> atonement, by the reason of life.

This atonement is the center of the Passover which will soon be celebrated far to the south in Jerusalem. Jesus seems to be claiming to have in His flesh and

JOHN 6:66-71

blood that power of atonement. Many of His *disciples* find this hard to accept. So they leave Him!

Jesus turns to the twelve that form the core of His disciples, asking if they too will desert Him in the Galilee. Peter, with hopes that this Joshua-Jesus will conquer the world still not diminished despite His puzzling words, proclaims Him to be the Holy One of God. That is a title for the Caesars who so completely dominate the country, be it in the name of Tiberias across the lake, Julias not far north of Capernaum, Caesarea of Philip the Tetrarch to the far north, Livias in the south, Sebaste in the heart of Samaria, or Caesarea on the coastal plain of the Great Sea. It is not the Caesars of Rome, however, but this Giver of Bread in Whom all hope has been placed, *Who is the Holy One of the true God.*

Yet, there is no consolation in the *Village of Comfort.* Instead of expressing satisfaction in this acclamation, Jesus points out that even among the remaining few there is a devil. He refers to Judah the son of Simon whose name well indicates the place of his origin. He is a citizen — "ish" as it is pronounced in Hebrew — of Cariot (hence, Iscariot). This town of merchants is on the main route running through the heart of the southern section of the former tribe of Judah. This area was given to the disgraced tribe of Simeon. That ally of Judah's *Gen. 49:5-7* is "Simon" in its shortened form. Judah, the only Judean from the homeland among the twelve, will join the murmurers from the South in betraying Jesus. Indeed, the Giver of Signs of a paradise to come, Who possesses all the Life that JOHN 7:1 barren, half-dead Judea longs for, does not dare to go about Judea, because the Judeans are seeking to kill Him. Instead, He waits for His *hour* traveling about the Galilee.

chapter seven

Blindness and Sight

The last time Jesus leaves the Galilee for Jerusalem He is alone. The pilgrim bands, including His disciples, are already in Jerusalem celebrating the Feast of Succoth, *Booths*. The harvest of fruits and vegetables is completed. It is time for the outpouring of joy-filled thanksgiving. However, as Jesus moves through the Jezreel Valley for the last time this October, there is a lonely emptiness about it — almost a sense of death in the air. Dust cones swirl across barren, unplowed fields that will not be worked again until after the first rains. Scattered through the fields are the remnants of the harvest — rotting fruit, vegetable stalks going to seed, and the dusty stubs of grain harvested months ago. The flocks along the way are noticeably smaller and the sheep thinner. A lonely hireling left to take care of the sheep and goats of families who have gone to the festival idles away his time, half caring about his charges. Villages which bustled during the harvest season look deserted. Many have left for the celebrations in Samaria and Judea. A short while ago, succoth, the makeshift *booths* erected in the fields to provide shelter from the sun during harvest, were filled with life, fun, and refreshment. Now they add to the impression of desolation as they are slowly torn apart by the wind.

JOHN 7:2-10 44

This eastern part of the Jezreel underscores the atmosphere of death by its tragic history. At the Spring of Harod, the first king, Saul, had begun the fight for his life only to be forced to commit suicide on Mount Gilboa above (rather than surrender to the hated Philistine forces who controlled the valley). His beloved son, Jonathan, also perished in that battle. As the former Bethshan is passed at the end of the valley, the last reminder in the Galilee is the grisly sight of Saul's decapitated body hanging from the wall of the city which was located where the pagan worship center Scythopolis now stands. What would be the end of the last King of God's People? Lonely is the way.

1 Sam. 28:3-25, 31:1-10

Two days later, after the southern end of the Jordan Valley is reached, Jesus passes through the groves near Jericho where young palm fronds were cut for the festival. The palm appropriately symbolizes the joy of the feast now in progress. This tree marks the oases in a desert land as it brings forth sustenance. Prayer for such life is central to the Feast of Succoth especially here in a land that has become bone-dry during six rainless months. Because of the scarcity of palms in the highlands about Jerusalem, many pilgrims have come to Jericho to cut branches for the festival. Each palm frond is bound together with three twigs of myrtle and two of willow to form a festive bouquet called in Hebrew, lulab, *palm-branch*. These water-loving plants are bound together not only by strands of willow or myrtle, but also by colorful threads. The rich even use gold and silver. This bouquet of greenery is waved during all the ceremonies, processions, and

Mishnah, Sukkah

Overleaf:
The last reminder in the Galilee is the grisly sight of Saul's decapitated body hanging from the wall of the city where the pagan acropolis of Scythopolis now stands... Lonely is the way. *(left)*

111

dances of Succoth, as a citron (a kind of large lemon), is held in the other hand.

Lev. 23:40 As the lulabim are waved this year in fulfillment of Moses' command, prayers will not only be offered for rain, but also for freedom from occupation when an anointed one will bring true life and joy.

Leaving behind the palm groves of Jericho, Jesus climbs to Jerusalem through the desert of whose blooming the People dream. He moves along the way which is waiting to be smoothed for the one expected to enter into Jerusalem in triumphant reply to the waving of lulabim and cries of Hosanna, *save us Lord*. He is alone.

In the Temple area, his destination, there is much singing and dancing. A jubilant crowd relaxes at the end of a hard year's labor. As they look over the city and hills surrounding them, the many booths perched on rooftops or set up in courtyards catch their eye. Since living space is always at a premium in Jerusalem, some pilgrims have set up their booths on the Mount of Olives. The *Lev. 23:41-43* booths are a reminder of the days of the Exodus and God's care for His People as they lived in makeshift homes in the desert. They are very simple — four poles supporting the frame of a roof over which are laid reeds, or branches of palms and willows, and even straw. The sides may be entirely closed, but the roof must be fashioned so that those who eat and sleep in it during the week-long feast will see the stars and the moon.

112

Of course, the succah or *booth,* is also a symbol of the farmer and his shelter during the harvest. This is particularly meaningful for urban dwellers so far removed from the soil. It helps the People recall that God brought their ancestors through the wilderness to a land which would flow with blessings only so long as they would properly care for it and depend on Him alone for the life-giving water. In joyous response to His goodness, the People take extra delight in adding fancy touches to their booths: colorful ribbons, flowers, or artfully twisted vines. There is an abundance of laughter and joking each evening to accompany the devouring of special Succoth treats, savoring of better wines, playing of games, singing of songs, and telling of many an amusing tale of the past year. To sleep outdoors in a booth is always a double treat for the children. Succoth is, like all the feasts of God's People, a real family affair.

Often during the festivities the People look to the way descending the Mount of Olives. An anointed one is expected to enter Jerusalem along that way to bring salvation as the prophets promised. When he appears on the final Succoth, the mount will be split in two from east to west so the king may enter in triumph riding on a donkey. The worshipers are prepared for that great moment when they will greet him with shouts of Hosanna and the waving of palms and lulabim.

Deut. 11:10-17

Zech. 9:9

Lower left: Succoth, the makeshift *Booths* erected in the fields to provide shelter from the sun during harvest.

A festive bouquet called in Hebrew, *lulab,* palm-branch.

Often during the festivities the People look to the way descending the Mount of Olives.

JOHN 7:11-13   Those gathered in the Temple area wonder if this new Worker of Signs and Wonders, Joshua-Jesus, will appear at the festival and fulfill their dreams. It is a hushed expectation, to be sure. Already His words and acts have so angered or disappointed some that, unbelievably, they seek to kill Him!

JOHN 7:14-44   Jesus arrives in the Temple area at the middle of the feast, the fourth day. He immediately accuses some of wanting to kill Him because He healed a man on the Sabbath last year at Succoth. To be sure, He also has quite a number of supporters who believe in Him because of the signs He has performed in Judea and the Galilee. These wonders, however, are immaterial to an opposition that knows exactly the conditions that the anointed one must fulfill. Jesus is disqualified immediately on geographical grounds. Everyone knows His place of origin, Nazareth in the half-pagan Galilee. Every day of Succoth, as the pilgrims

Zech. 12:7-19   pass the beautifully adorned tomb of the great king David, they recall that the anointed one will be from that royal line. He will hail from that small farm village

Micah 5:2   five miles south of Jerusalem, Bethlehem of Judea. Jesus does not enter into the debate that swirls around Him. He does not want to be equated with an earthly David, for in the beginning He came from above.

114

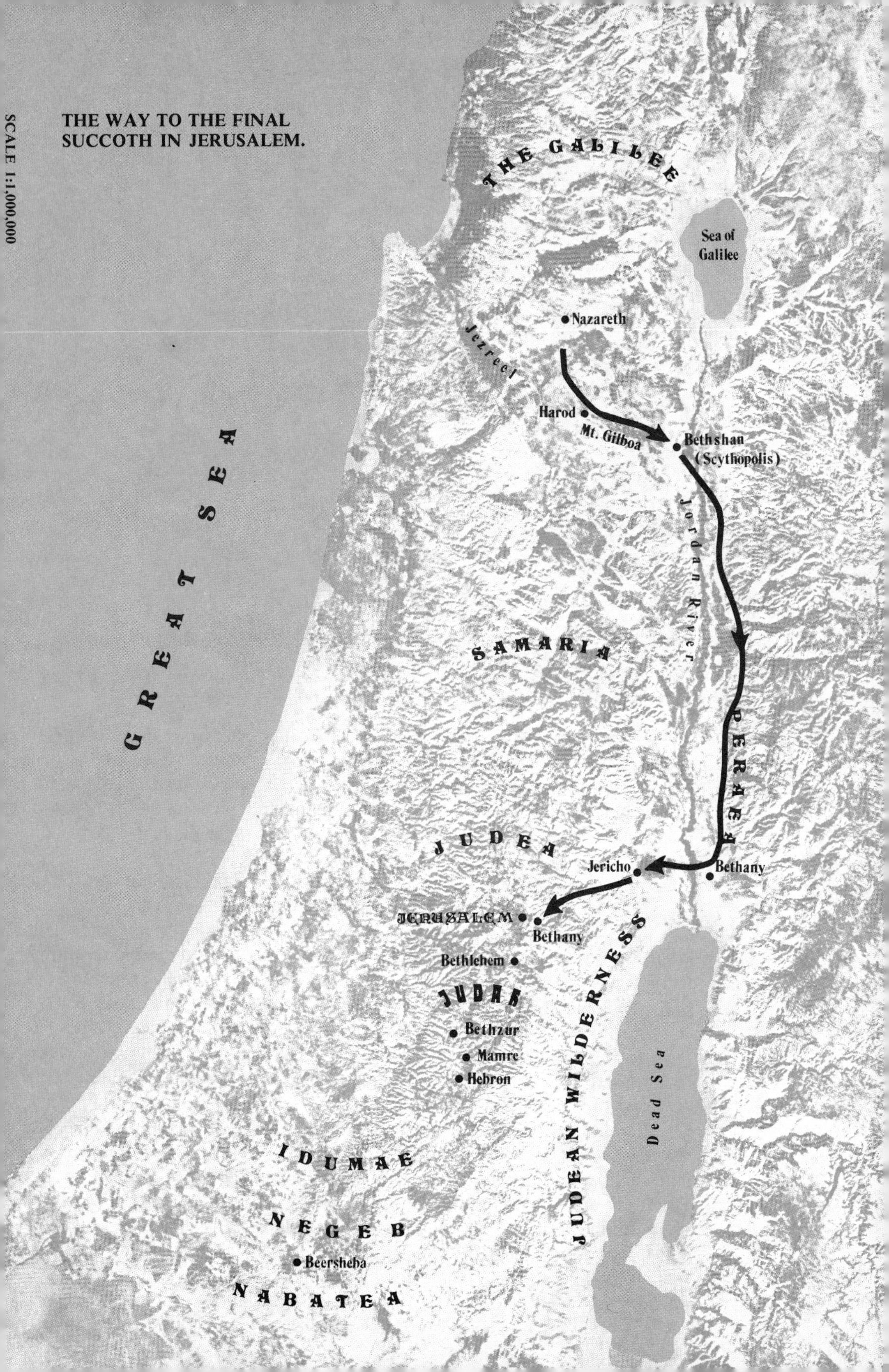

THE WAY TO THE FINAL
SUCCOTH IN JERUSALEM.

SCALE 1:1,000,000

THE GALILEE

Sea of
Galilee

Nazareth

Jezreel

Harod
Mt. Gilboa

Bethshan
(Scythopolis)

Jordan River

GREAT SEA

SAMARIA

PERAEA

JUDEA

Jericho

Bethany

JERUSALEM

Bethany

Bethlehem

JUDEAN WILDERNESS

JUDAH

Bethzur

Mamre

Hebron

Dead Sea

IDUMAE

NEGEB

Beersheba

NABATEA

Water empties into the Pool of Siloam from a tunnel which connects it with the Spring of Gihon.

JOHN 7:45-52

As the festival week draws to a close, Temple police sent by the chief priests and leaders of the Pharisees to arrest Jesus, return empty-handed — but excited by His fantastic words spoken at the climax of the feast. Although His words were completely unexpected, they seem to be the fulfillment of all the hopes of the People at this feast. This becomes especially clear when they are reflected on in terms of the daily ritual of the Feast of Succoth.

Each morning priests gather around the altar after the first burnt sacrifice of the day. After circling the altar as they sing psalms and wave the lulabim, a priest takes a golden pitcher and leads the other priests in procession through the gate leading from the Men's Court. After crossing over the Temple area and passing through a Huldah Gate, they descend through the former City of David to the Pool of Siloam. The pitcher is then filled with the pool's precious water.

2 Chron. 32:1-4

The Pool of Siloam is fed from the Spring of Gihon, the source of water for Jerusalem. Hezekiah cut a 1,750-foot tunnel under the City and built the pool for better protection of its crucial water supply. The source to which Siloam's waters flow is a most peculiar spring. Gihon means *gush* in Hebrew, which is exactly what the spring does. Several times each day at intervals of four to ten hours, the spring *gushes* water for 30 or 40 minutes and then recedes. Why? Some claim that Isaiah, whose tomb stands just above the Pool of Siloam, controls its waters. The origin of the Gihon Spring is not difficult to determine. The location of the spring (in the Kidron Valley south of the Temple Mount) allows water to seep into it from the area of the altar stone high above. Gihon's water is blessed.

Because one of the rivers of paradise was called Gihon, some would even claim that the waters flowing into the Pool of Siloam are actually a remnant of the paradise whose return is prayed for at Succoth. Into this blessed water, the priest dips the golden pitcher and turns to carry the water back to its origin, the altar. The People pray for such a continuing cycle of blessing for the land. *Gen. 2:13*

Crowds gather on either side of the way as the grand procession returns to the Temple. The line of priests moves at a stately pace as the golden pitcher sparkles in the sun and row after row of white robes billow in the breeze. There is the accompanying swish of hundreds of waving branches fanning the air. The *Ps. 120-134* hills about Jerusalem resound with the festive shouts of joyous pilgrims singing the Psalms of the Ascents. The doors of a Huldah Gate are wide open as the priests enter to ascend to the great platform. Upon their arrival above they are greeted with a burst of cheers, blasts of trumpets, and shouts of hosanna! Moving through the sea of waving lulabim they pass the barricade that prevents pagans from witnessing the climax of the week-long celebration. After they enter the packed Men's Court, the priest climbs the ramp leading to the top of the altar. Others who have been waiting with specially cut willow branches lay them beside the altar or wave them wildly in the air. The song of Succoth rings out as the throng pressing around the altar wave their lulabim for the last time.

> This is the day which the Lord has made; *Ps. 118:24-25*
> let us rejoice and be glad in it.
> Hosanna, *Save us, we beseech thee, O Lord!*

At this moment, amidst the brilliant array of colorful garments, waving greenery, and the shouts of joyous acclamation, the priest pours the water from *Zec. 14:8* the golden pitcher onto the altar. This symbolizes the prayer that not only rain and dew will come in the new year, but that the river of paradise will flow from *Ezek. 47:1-12* the side of the altar, quenching all thirst. To underscore this prayer for the fertility of the land and life for the People, the worshipers bend and beat the earth with their willows. At this culmination of the feast Jesus cries out:

> If any one thirst, let him come to Me and drink. *John 7:37-38*
> He who believes in Me, as the Scripture has said
> *out of Him will flow rivers of living water.*

The Galilean Who two Passovers ago proclaimed Himself the Sanctuary, now claims to be the altar rock from whose side the paradisaical stream will flow. He is the fulfillment of *the* feast, Succoth. He is *the* Source of Life for the thirsting ones who long to be free.

This claim stuns the Temple police sent to arrest Him. How could they take *JOHN 7:47-52* Him into custody? Nobody had ever spoken like this at a previous Succoth. The leaders of the Pharisees rebuke them. They, the educated of God's People, not the crowd, know better than to be impressed by His words. Nicodemus, who is *John 3:1, 10* one of the learned, does try to speak in defense of Jesus only to be chided with the accusation of becoming a *Galilean.* He has been so blinded by this Northerner that he forgets that the Judeans are those who truly understand the Scripture

117

and proper worship of God. Besides, any educated person knows that the prophet like Moses is not to come from the North.

The opponents of Jesus are concerned about His talk of departing for a place where these Judeans cannot find Him. Could it be that His message will be taken home by the pilgrims from distant lands, then followed by His coming to them? These members of the Diaspora have a poor grasp of the true meaning of Scripture because they know so little Hebrew. They study Scripture in Greek, opening the way to many possible misunderstandings. They are even labeled "Greeks" because of their use of the world's language. How tragic it would be if Jesus were allowed to carry His teaching to those "Greeks." *John 7:32-36*

Meanwhile, a crowd has gathered in the Women's Court (also called the Treasury because of the trumpet-shaped collection boxes placed at its entrance) to listen to His inspiring message. There could be no better place for a popular preacher to gather a congregation. In this area *all* of God's People — male and female, Judean, Samaritan, Galilean, Greek, Nazarene, and even the lepers who come here for certification that they are healed — can hear His message. The Rabbi's words cause those about Him to reconsider the meaning of the wonderful nights they have spent in this court during the past week. *JOHN 8:12-30*

Each night of the feast, four gigantic stands are set up in each corner of the Women's Court. On the arms of the stands huge bowls filled with olive oil are placed. Thousands of wicks made from the discarded undergarments of the priests float in the bowls. These are set ablaze as the festival throng gathers each night. They give out so much light that the night of the court seems to turn to day. In fact, the light emanating from Jerusalem is so intense that it can be seen from outlying villages. This is a sign that on the final Succoth, night and darkness will disappear from the world. Only the first created light will remain. *Zech. 14:7*

Gen. 1:3-4

Dancers with torches enter into the bright glow of the gigantic lamps. Accompanied by harp, pipe, trumpet, drum, and cymbal they dance on the steps leading from the Women's Court to the Nicanor Gate, the entrance to the Men's Court and altar area. On each of the 15 steps they perform a torch dance to one of the Psalms of the Ascents. The polished bronze of the Nicanor Gate provides a flaming background for them as it reflects the torches' flickering light. The revelry continues until just before the sun rises over the Mount of Olives. Then suddenly it is stopped by three blasts of the trumpets. The worshipers make way as the Nicanor Gate is opened and the priests walk through them and proceed to the eastern entrance of the Women's Court, the Beautiful Gate. There they turn their backs on the rising sun, crying out as they face the Sanctuary: *Ps. 120-134*

Our fathers when they were in this place
turned with their backs toward the Temple of
the Lord and their faces toward the east,
and worshiped the sun toward the east; but as for us,
our eyes are turned toward the Lord.

Mishnah, Sukkah 5:4

As the sun's rays stream over the Mount of Olives turning the white facade of the Sanctuary with its gold and silver plates into such a brilliant source of light that they must shield their eyes, they again repeat the refrain: "Our eyes are

Left:
Each night of the feast four gigantic stands are set up in each corner of the Women's Court.

119

turned toward the Lord." With that wonderful confessional moment fresh in mind, those gathered about Jesus now hear Him proclaim as He stands between the Temple and the place of the sun's rising:

John 8:12

> I am the Light of the world;
> he who follows Me will never
> walk in darkness, but will have
> the Light of Life.

John 1:4-5

He claims to be that first Light that goes beyond sun, moon, or a light-reflecting building. He is the Illumination signed by the nights of Succoth Who brings Light into a darkened world.

His opponents are exasperated and angered by His teaching. They accuse Him of bearing witness only to Himself, and before God's House at that! Jesus agrees. He is indeed pointing to Himself because His Father bears witness, and points to Him as the Center of His Glory. Then again, many are not disturbed by His claim. These Judeans have believed in Him.

JOHN 8:31-33

As He continues, the response of these believing Judeans is rather odd. When He tells them that their continuing as His disciples will free them, they deny that they have ever been in bondage. Their lack of knowledge of the trials of the fathers after Abraham is incomprehensible. Abraham, in fact, was shown the

Gen. 15:13

bondage of his seed in Egypt on the stone forming the base of the altar rising before them! Even more, how is it possible to make such a claim as they stand in the courts of the Temple in occupied Jerusalem? Their refusal to acknowledge what they see about them is inexcusable. They must be blind!

Overshadowing the Temple is the Roman barracks, the Antonia. Now that the feast is over, the high priest must return his garments to that control center to be kept under lock and key by Rome! If one but glances past the barrier excluding pagans from the Sanctuary, one must certainly catch sight of a Roman soldier or two on patrol. Nor is that barrier a real blockade against Rome's influence at the altar itself. The high priest, Caiaphas, officiates here *only* because Rome appointed and approved him. If these believing Judeans just turn their eyes to the left of God's House, they must see the residence of the executor of Caesar's commands towering over the heights of the city. God's People are far from free. These believers in Jesus are simply not admitting to the stark reality confronting them.

JOHN 8:34-38

Jesus continues by carrying His followers' thoughts south to the barren Negeb and the area of Abraham's dwelling by Beersheba. They know that the slave's son, Ishmael, did not remain in Father Abraham's house. The true son, Isaac, remained forever. Jesus, the true Son, promises to give freedom to His

Gen. 21:2-21

followers. These alone are the true descendants of Isaac. Jesus accuses His Judean disciples, however, of being just like Ishmael who tried to kill Isaac at Beersheba. This was the reason for Ishmael's expulsion and near death in the

Midrash Rabbah
Gen. 53:11

desert of the Negeb. His *playing* with Isaac is understood as his attempts to kill the free-born son. This insult stings His followers as they look out over the Temple area and see some of those detested, pagan Nabateans from the far south who are thought to be the sons of Ishmael. These Ishmaelites have killed many of

120

God's People in the past. Their presence in Jerusalem is tolerated because of the precious goods they so expertly transport across the great desert of Arabia — and because they are very good friends of Rome.

Mamre near Hebron, where that beautiful open-air shrine most recently renovated by Herod the Great is situated.

JOHN 8:39-50

Gen. 18:1-8

John 8:41

The claim of the believing Judeans that they are the seed of Abraham is not challenged by Jesus, for so was Ishmael. They act exactly like him rather than his father, the Patriarch. Abraham never contemplated murder. At Mamre near Hebron, where that beautiful open-air shrine most recently renovated by Herod the Great is situated, pilgrims continue to remember his great work of hospitality. Here he gave food and drink to the three angels.

These believers can no longer bear His barbs. They answer with a terrible accusation, "We were not born of fornication!" It is as if a long simmering rumor can no longer be hidden. Jesus was born of an unwed mother. They know that God is their heavenly Father. Stories of virgin births they do not need.

Jesus rejects their claim to be children of God because they show no love for Him Who is from God. This can only mean they are sons of the devil. Like their satan-possessed father, they are murderers and (as their false claim to be free makes clear) liars. They are so deep in sin they will not hear His words.

This onslaught calls forth yet another counterattack by His followers — He is a Samaritan! Did He not move from Judea to become mixed with the corrupted remnant of Israel far from this center of true worship? He has allowed Himself to be polluted by these half-pagans as they proclaimed Him the Savior of the world. He is not of God, they conclude, but demon-possessed!

121

Abraham's tomb at Hebron, the greatest monument to death in the land.

JOHN 8:51-55

Gen. 25:7-10

The white heat of this crossfire right in the middle of the holiest place on earth is shocking. Yet Jesus continues to feed their anger by claiming that those who keep His Word will never see death. His words carry the thoughts of His adversaries south to the greatest monument to death in the land, Abraham's tomb at Hebron. Herod the Great had enclosed this sacred site in an open-air, high-walled shrine which is magnificent in its simple, finely-cut stonework. Here is visible proof of the death which faces all of Abraham's seed. Certainly Jesus would not, indeed could not, claim to be greater than Father Abraham. His monument attests to the reality and finality of death, as do the numerous tombs of the prophets in Judea. These extend from Hebron to the very entrance of the

2 Kings 22:14-20

John 1:14

Temple area where the prophetess Huldah is buried. Who then does Jesus claim to be? He replies that He, Who truly knows God, is the Glory of God that once rested in the tabernacle in the wilderness and, later, on this very mount. To make

Ex. 40:34

any less a claim would make Him a liar like them.

JOHN 8:56-5*7*

Jesus points to the altar which has been the focus of Succoth. This has been a place of joy from the days of Abraham who, Judeans believe, was the first to offer sacrifices here. God commanded Abraham to offer on this rock each of the animals that would later be sacrificed before His House: heifer, she-goat, ram

Gen. 15:1-21

turtledove, and young pigeon. He had cut these in two, as God directed, laying each side across from the other on top of the rock upon which the altar now stands. The birds were not divided, but laid facing each other. As darkness approached, a flame and smoking fire pot passed between the pieces. In this

Midrash Rabbah Gen. 44:22

mystical moment, Abraham saw the future of his descendants and even the Anointed One! With joy he had witnessed that *day* of the final sacrifice which would bring freedom and paradise to his seed. Before this memory-filled place, Jesus proclaims that Abraham rejoiced because he saw His *day*.

JOHN 8:58-59

The believing Judeans cannot begin to comprehend what He is talking about! How can someone who has never been in Abraham's bosom (that is, died) possibly have seen Abraham? Jesus' reply seems blasphemous. He claims to have been "before Abraham!" He is making Himself equal to God! The enraged believers grab for fragments left from the constuction work in the court to stone this blasphemer.

Their action is reminiscent of what originally happened here. Legend recalls that when Abraham came to sacrifice Isaac on this rock, rejoicing to fulfill God's terrible command, he saw a little old man in the distance walking slowly toward them. As he drew nearer, Abraham was frightened because he clutched a stone in his hand. The Patriarch knew immediately that this was no son of Adam, but the devil himself coming to defile the perfect sacrifice of his son. He quickly picked up Isaac and ran to the grotto under the rock of sacrifice and hid him. Thus he kept the offering of his son unblemished and acceptable for the right time of sacrifice. Thus these sons of the devil would defile God's Only Son before the *hour* of sacrifice comes. Before they can carry out their design, Jesus runs from the court, evading His pursuers as He loses Himself in the great throng leaving the Temple area by the grand stairway of the Royal Porch.

Gen. 22:9-14

Midrash Rabbah Gen. 56:5

John 3:16

Jesus and the twelve who have followed Him leave the stairway and enter the marketplace at the southwest corner of the Temple Mount. They pass one of the many beggars who hope someone entering the Temple will have mercy and drop a coin or two in their hands. The poor fellow is blind. The disciples ask Jesus whose sin was the cause of the blindness which has been with this man since birth. Jesus explains it has nothing to do with sin, but rather is to make known the Glory of God. Proclaiming again that He is the Light of the world, He gathers some dirt, forms it into a mudpack with His spittle and smears it on the man's eyes. Then He *sends* him down to the Pool of Siloam to wash. Immediately he responds to Jesus' command and descends through the former City of David, the same way the priests had gone every morning of Succoth.

JOHN 9:1-41

Shiloah, the original Hebrew form of Siloam, means *sent*. Legend claims that its waters were *sent* by God to quench the thirst of Isaiah during his martyrdom in the King's Garden, not far from Siloam. Isaiah, in turn, now *sends* the water of Gihon Spring to the Siloam Pool, providing a remnant of paradise for God's thirsting People. Where the priest had dipped the empty golden pitcher into the pool so that this sign of life might be brought back to the altar, the blind one dips his head, washes his eyes, and sees! Isaiah's tomb above this scene reminds one of his question: "Who has believed our report, and to whom has the arm of the Lord been revealed?" That question now is answered. The sighted one starts back toward the Temple area, ascending the way along which God's

Ascension of Isaiah 5:1-14

Is. 53:1

John 12:38

Overleaf:
He calls his own sheep by name and leads them out.
Below:
The Royal Porch

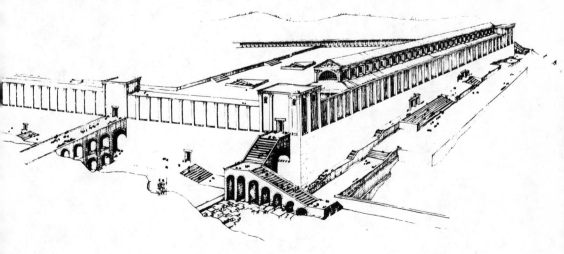

People had gathered to cry out for salvation during Succoth. The joy of that salvation wells up in him, for he now *sees the way!*

How great the difference between this Succoth healing by the life-giving waters of Siloam and that last year by the shrine of Asclepius-Serapis next to the stagnant waters of the Sheep Pool. This man responds to Jesus' words and acts in faith, unlike the cripple at Bethzatha on the other side of the Temple, who had JOHN 9:8-12 everything done for him. That ungrateful man did not even know Who had healed him, while this former blind man thankfully explains to his acquaintances that his Healer's name is Jesus, although he does not know where He is.

JOHN 9:13-23 Like the man at Bethzatha, he is then questioned by Pharisees because his healing also took place on a Sabbath. In fact, Jesus anointed his eyes by the corner tower of the Temple area from which the trumpeter announces the beginning of Sabbath.

The Pharisees are divided. Some condemn such an act of mercy as a violation of the Sabbath. Others see this deed as a sign of Jesus' goodness. The former blind man does not hesitate to enter the debate. He proclaims Jesus a prophet! The man's parents, however, act more like the cripple at Bethzatha. They fear expulsion from the synagogue if they become involved.

JOHN 9:24-34 During his second session with these questioning Judeans, the man who now has his sight grows even bolder. Not only does he retell his story, but he begins to do some missionary work as well. He invites these Pharisees to become Jesus' disciples too! That invitation is rejected, for they are disciples of Moses. This does not discourage the man whose insight becomes ever clearer. He presses his arguments further. They should know from where Jesus comes and Whose will He does since He can open the eyes of a man born blind. Jesus, the Prophet and Giver of Sight, must be from God. That profession is too much for his listeners, who immediately expel him from their synagogue.

JOHN 9:35-41 Jesus comes to the man to whom He has given sight, just as He sought out the healed cripple in the Temple area last year. With this one healed by Siloam's living water there is no talk of sin, only the question of the depth of his faith. His question as to the Healer's identity is answered by Jesus simply replying that he *has seen.* Instead of bending to pick up stones as the Judeans who believed in Him had done, the newly sighted man responds by bowing in worship. The outcast of the synagogue now sees the real Holy Place is in this outcast of the Temple.

The Pharisees, who through their questioning showed their ever-deepening blindness, are now clearly judged by Jesus. The ones who are blind now see, and those who claim to see are made blind. Isaiah's thoughts concerning blindness and sight echo in Jesus' words, as complete healing has come from the pool beneath the prophet's resting place. Isaiah had spoken of this moment of Light Is. 6:1-13 coming into darkness and those rejecting it. In his visions in the Sanctuary, and John 12:40-41 during his martyrdom in the King's Garden not far from Siloam, he, like Father Abraham, had seen the *day* of Jesus. He also foresaw the growing opposition to this Light which would bring about the *day.*

Right:
The porch is named Solomon's because part of its base is clearly older than Herod's structure.

Jesus explains that He is the Shepherd for those who will see. He reminds the questioning Pharisees of the hirelings taking care of the flocks while their owners are in Jerusalem for the feast. The true shepherd, not the hireling, is the

126

During the eight
days of Hanukkah
eight lamps are lit
and placed in
windows or on
stands by
entrance ways.

JOHN 10:1-21

one that sheep trustfully follow to the watering and feeding places during these terribly dry days. Jesus proclaims that He is that good Shepherd of God's People. He is not like these hirelings who do not care for members of His flock, like this former blind man. He is ready, as the Good Shepherd, to lay down His life on the *day* for His flock. On that *day* the Good Shepherd will become the Lamb of sacrifice for the People.

His words leave a divided People after Succoth. To some His words sound like nonsense. To others His words are too powerful to be rejected, for they are spoken by One Whom they saw turn a way of darkness into a way of Light.

JOHN 10:22

1 Maccabees 4:26-59

2 Maccabees 10

Ps. 118:24-25

Light coming into a darkened world is the theme of the feast which takes place in the rain-filled days of December. The Feast of Hanukkah, *Dedication,* marks the fulfillment of the prayers of Succoth, not only for the blessing of the life-giving rain, but also for the coming of the Lord's deliverance from oppression. Almost two centuries ago at the village of Bethzur by the Hebron road, Judas Maccabee defeated the pagan force that had snuffed out the light in the Holy Place as it attempted to force heathen beliefs on the People. God gave Judas the success prayed for in the Hosanna of Succoth. He returned to Jerusalem in triumph and cleansed the Temple, re-*dedicating* it. Palm branches, which are also waved at Hanukkah, symbolize the answering of the prayers of Succoth. Indeed, this feast is referred to as a second Succoth.

Josephus, Antiquities
XII, 325
1 Kings 8

During the eight days of this winter festival, eight lamps are lit and placed in windows or on stands by entrance ways. This is to remind the People of the relighting of the lamps in God's House when all seemed so dark in the face of the overwhelming enemy. For this reason Hanukkah is also called the Feast of Lights.

During one of the feast days Jesus finds shelter from the cold winter wind and rain in the Porch of Solomon, located on the eastern side of the Temple area. The porch is so named because part of its base is clearly older than Herod's structure. It is thought to date from the original Temple platform of Solomon. This king's *dedication* of the first House of God is also remembered at the Feast of Lights.

Judeans soon gather around Jesus, pressing Him at this feast of the expected culmination of the Succoth hopes for life and light to declare if He is indeed the anointed one, the shepherd of the People like the long-expected son of David. Jesus protests that He has made clear Who He is. Yet, they will not believe because they are not of His sheep. Now, as at Succoth, He fulfills the answer to the Succoth prayers. At this Feast of Dedication of the Holy Place *John 2:21* which He now has replaced, He proclaims that He and the Father are One. Again they pick up stones in order to snuff out this blasphemer's life. As at JOHN 10:31-39 Succoth, He forces His way through the crowd, escaping from those who will only celebrate the *dedication* of a building.

His escape route is the familiar way to Jericho. This is the way of hope that priests and Levites descended in the beginning in order to question the Baptist. JOHN 10:40-42 John's answer had been to point to this One Who now removes Himself from the cold, dark days of a Jerusalem winter and enters into the warmth and light of Bethany of Peraea. Here He is welcomed by the winter crowds that once had *John 1:19* followed John. Now they see a Light Who far outshines the single burning lamp *John 5:35* of the one who prepared the way, or the blazing lights of Hanukkah. They see One Who is Succoth's Life and Light.

chapter eight

The Seventh Sign

In the darkness of the day, before the dawning of light over Bethany below in the Jordan Valley or Bethany above by the Mount of Olives, Lazarus, the brother of Mary and Martha, grows weaker as sickness hurries him toward death. The sisters who love and are so loved by Jesus immediately dispatch one of the strong, fleet-footed youth of the village to race down to the other Bethany in Peraea to fetch the Rabbi Who alone can prevent that tragedy.

JOHN 11:1-3-16

Engulfed in a world that is still more darkness than light, the messenger leaves the ridge behind the village for the steep descent to Jericho. The path that descends through the shallow valley and crosses a field to the junction with the way from Jerusalem is familiar enough to the messenger so that he can avoid stumbling in the dim light. When the sun rises over the hills east of the Jordan Valley, he is moving rapidly along the fairly even section of the way which has been built up and into the side of the hills on his right. His effort, however, has already become unnecessary. Lazarus has lost his struggle with death.

Wailing cries echo through Bethany. Neighbors begin to gather at the home as the messenger emerges from the hillside way and catches his first view of the other Bethany. Leaving behind the inn and fort complex which overlooks the dangerous central section of the road immediately in front of him, he descends and crosses this low-lying section. The bright sun now shining in his face forces him to shield his eyes.

In Bethany the eyes of Lazarus are closed and his body bathed. Olive oil mixed with perfume is tenderly rubbed over it. The sisters' thoughts often turn to Jesus. If He had stayed, so their distraught thoughts might run, Lazarus would be a living brother whom they could rub with soothing oils rather than a dead brother to be anointed for burial. They tend to forget that Jesus' retreat is His own fight to escape premature death! Long, thin bands of linen cloth are now wound around the body, binding the legs and arms close to its side. Spices are carefully bound between the layers of the bandage-like wrappings. This will not help preserve the body, but will veil the odor of corrupting death. As the bands reach Lazarus' neck, the sisters are overcome, shuddering with grief. They gaze for the last time at his face which is only a waxen likeness of the warm features they had so often caressed. After the chin is bound in place by a band of cloth tied around the head, a finely woven linen cloth is fastened over the head. They weep.

Head held high, legs striding, and arms swinging to increase his speed, the messenger seems to draw on a reserve of energy as he tackles the last part of the

Left:
The messenger leaves the ridge behind Bethany for the steep descent to Jericho.

way. Bethany is now clearly visible across from Jericho. Soon he can convey his call for life and the great Healer can hasten up to Bethany to prevent the triumph of death.

They are now ready to bear the body to the grave. As the mourners gather in and about the sisters' home, they begin the customary litany of discordant chants, prayers, and lamentations. The sisters are supported in their grief as the whole village turns out to accompany them in the slow walk down through the village and over to the graveyard. The wrapped body resting on a simple stretcher is carried first. The sisters follow. The men walk behind them in two rows, a sadly broken and depressed group accompanied by the mournful melody of flutes. Finally, rows of lamenting village women follow, wringing their hands, beating their breasts, and tearing at their hair. A tomb chamber has long before been cut into the low hillside facing Bethany. They gather about the small, square opening just large enough for the body to pass through. Hands lift in final prayer. Then the bound body is moved from the light of late morning into the gloomy darkness of the small chamber. The ceiling of the tomb is not more than five and a half feet high, just high enough to allow those receiving the body to stand as they lay it on one of the three benches cut around the sides facing the small opening.

The process of decay will take place in this humid darkness until only dust *Gen. 3:19* and powdery bone fragments remain. This is the final sign of death's victory — man returned to dust. Later these remains will be placed into a small receptacle, an ossuary, as the bench is cleared to receive another body. Several high-necked perfume jars are passed into the chamber and their contents sprinkled over the body. More spices are also packed about the corpse, combining with the already heavily perfumed wrappings to give a sickening-sweet smell to this place of final sleep. Finally, more oil is poured into the lamp resting in the niche above the body. This is a symbol of the hope that there will be light at the end of this long *Josephus, War II, 162-163* night of darkness. Lazarus and his family are Pharisees. They hope for the resurrection of the dead on the last day when the light of resurrecting dew will *Is. 26:19* come to this land of the shades. Left in the dull twilight, the body is tightly sealed from the world of the living. An evenly cut square slab of limestone with a thick, projecting center on one side is fitted into the niche-like borders about the opening. The tomb is closed.

At long last the exhausted messenger arrives at the light-bathed valley floor and heads across the Jordan River. At Bethany in Peraea he reports that Lazarus is failing quickly. He pleads on behalf of the sisters that Jesus come immediately. It is not yet the sixth hour. There is still enough time to hurry back to the ailing Lazarus in Bethany before total darkness overtakes the most dangerous part of the way. By torchlight it will still be possible to reach the *JOHN 11:4-5* village by the second watch of the night. Jesus makes no response except to comment that this sickness will not end in death!

Meanwhile, Mary and Martha return to their home to begin the week of mourning. They sit on the floor with women mourners around them. The men gather in another room, or sit outside in the midday sun. Occasionally the sisters go to the ridge just above the village where in the clear winter air they can see the other Bethany far below them. They imagine Jesus rushing to leave the valley.

Left:
Even in broad daylight they have nearly stumbled over the flints and pebbles scattered over so many sections of the road.

133

The burial was in
the Herodium
palace which rests
on a hill Herod
had raised to its
present height.

He will come soon. To be sure, it will no longer be to heal but to comfort and support them in their mourning.

For two full days Jesus gives no indication of planning to leave the other Bethany. For two long days the sisters keep coming to the ridge above the village to stare down to where they know He is staying. Their bitterness grows as they gaze in bewilderment at that comfortable place of refuge He has chosen in full view of them.

JOHN 11:6-16

On the fourth day after the death of Lazarus, Jesus announces to the twelve that they should prepare to leave for Bethany. His disciples are not only surprised but dumbfounded. Why should they cross from Peraea into Judea? Did not the inhabitants of the southern part of the country, the Judeans, just now attempt to stone Him? Jesus answers rather obliquely that the twelve daylight hours (no matter what time of year, the period of sunlight is always perfectly divided into twelve) must be used for walking because, in the darkness of night, one will stumble. He, of course, refers to being in His Light. The disciples are not comforted. They can only think of that rugged way to Jerusalem. Even in broad daylight they have nearly stumbled over the flints and pebbles scattered over so many sections of the road. One does not promenade up to Jerusalem, but rather proceeds with one eye glued to the path to make sure of each succeeding step. Travel at night along that desert way is almost impossible, not because it is

134

unfamiliar, but rather because of the constant shifting of the small stones. They can cause a twisted ankle or even a broken leg.

Their confusion grows when Jesus further informs them that Lazarus is asleep. He wants to go and wake him! They look at the forbidding Mount of Olives far removed from them in the cold, cloud-covered highlands of Judea. They look around to the warm and safe Jordan Valley and try to reason with their Rabbi. If Lazarus has fallen asleep, they have no need to rush up there. What is a more perfect sign that the struggle against death has been victorious than when thrashing in fevered pain is calmed and healing sleep enfolds the sick. Everything will be all right. There is no need to jeopardize their own lives with a courtesy call at this point! Jesus then explains that by *sleep* He means that Lazarus is dead. Their bewilderment is complete when Jesus further explains that they must go there so that they might believe. Thomas, *Twin,* mirrors well the mood of the twelve as he sarcastically mutters to his fellow disciples, "Let us also go, that we may die with Him!"

The beginning of the way is easy. The morning sun is not yet at its zenith. The terrain is flat and free of obstacles. However, immediately after Jericho's palaces are passed, the way suddenly becomes steep and difficult. This path is the same one taken by the funeral procession of the king of the Judeans, Herod the Great. People still talk about how he was carried up this steep way on a golden bier, his body covered by a purple robe and his head bedecked with a

The cooling shade and shadow also refresh Jesus and His flock as they walk just below the sun-blocking ridge top.

Josephus, Antiquities
XVII, 194-195

diadem and golden crown. His scepter, the symbol of power bestowed upon him by mighty Rome, lay in his hand. His family surrounded the bier. Behind, in perfectly ordered rows came the troops. They represented the world from Gaul to Arabia as Rome honored the king of Judeans. They were dressed in polished armor which, reflecting the sun, gave the slow-paced lines the appearance of a daylight torch parade. Behind them several hundred servants carried spices to mask the stench of death. In cadence with the steady beat of the drums, the procession climbed to Jerusalem and then moved to the Herodium near Bethlehem. The burial was in the palace which rests on a hill Herod had raised to its present height above the other buildings. He prepared his final resting place in a form similar to his great benefactor, Augustus Caesar.

John 1:49

As the disciples look to the Rabbi (Who like themselves is breathing heavily and sweating from the demanding climb) they note how unlike the expected anointed one is He Whom Nathanael once triumphantly hailed as King of Israel back in Bethany. Even in death when a great king of the Judeans went this way, he appeared every inch a king, majestically borne aloft as the world marched at his side. The twelve struggle along behind One they fear is surely heading toward death. How common and helpless they seem. Their Leader is dressed drably in a simple, seamless tunic. He carries His robe which is useless in this warm region, even in midwinter. Straggling behind Him is no perfectly drilled army, but a small rag-tag group, some with tunics pulled up and tucked into their belts to give more freedom to their legs. Some lag further behind as the steep grade takes its toll. They rest for awhile after reaching the top of this initial incline, with Cyprus rising menacingly above them.

2 Sam. 19:1-20:2

As they look over the plain they have left behind, they can see the area of Gilgal north of the sprawling city of Jericho. There David returned from exile before he followed this way to Jerusalem to regain his power. However, the road to which the disciples now turn as they continue their climb was really no victory way for David, whom a forgetful People laud as God's son. At Gilgal, the tribe of Judah (originally south of the way Jesus now travels) and Israel (just across the valley) could find no reconciliation. With the cry of a Benjaminite, "Everyone to your tents, Oh, Israel," the kingdom split. David, betrayed by his most trusted counselor, and facing the task of uniting an impossibly divided People of God, slowly made his way up to Jerusalem.

The disciples continue along that route which begins to weave through the hilltops forming the sides of the deep valley beside them. They are well aware of the sharp division Jesus has caused among the People. David rode his mule along this way with the crack troops of Judah surrounding and supporting him as he returned to a safe Jerusalem from which he could reestablish his power base. In stark contrast, the disciples and their trusted Shepherd are on foot and completely alone as they approach a foreboding Jerusalem.

Right:
They are roused
from their
daydreams by the
desert's dramatic
sweep up to the
Mount of Olives.

The way is now a bit easier as the grade slackens. This provides a welcome opportunity to recoup one's strength! Flocks of nimble-footed goats can be seen climbing up and down the steep valley sides as they seek out the winter grass. They enjoy the cooling shade and shadow which also refresh Jesus and His flock as they walk just below the sun-blocking ridge top. They realize that this relieving shade can also be a shadow of death. This is why they often struggle up and over

Ps. 23
the peaks on this already steep way to Jerusalem. From these high vantage points, travelers can spot lurking bandits more easily. Rome, of course, has attempted to prevent this danger by building obvservation posts along the way. These are also needed to prevent guerrilla attacks from revolutionaries.

The disciples look across the valley to the rolling desert which provides sparse pasture at this time of year, and see a shepherd leading a line of sheep. Each member of the tightly ordered, single file line can at least catch a glimpse of the shepherd's stick as he looks above the fat tail of the sheep in front of him. This reassures him. He trusts his leader and travels the way to safety. Yet, the disciples' Shepherd, Who walks as usual in front of them with the line of His followers moving steadily behind, is leading them not to safety but rather to danger.

As the way leaves the edge of the valley the disciples come to a large cistern where sheep and weary travelers alike are watered. Its still water does not taste like that of the spring flowing in the valley far below their resting place, but in these desert hills it seems even more precious. Here they are nourished by a simple meal.

Although the disciples are refreshed by the water, food, and rest, their spirits lag as the Shepherd rises and continues to lead His flock up to Jerusalem. This part of the way is especially boring. The Mount of Olives, which has been visible all morning, disappears behind the rise in front of them and the deep valley is hidden by the hills on their right. There are only dust and stones on all sides. These, in turn, blend into a monotonous roll of barren hills sprinkled with a few scraggly thorn bushes. The dulling roadway induces reflection on previous exciting ways where signs, wonders, cheers, and an overflowing abundance of life had been daily fare.

As they trudge up the steep grade to the Roman fort and inn complex near the halfway point, they are roused from their daydreams by the dramatic sweep of the desert up to the Mount of Olives. For the first time since leaving Bethany of Peraea, they see their destination, Bethany of Judea. This second half of the way is discouraging, every bit as steep or steeper than the first half. Worse yet, there is not a steady incline to the Mount of Olives. The way is divided between the part which suddenly *descends* before them and then begins rolling over hill and dale, and the last part which rises steeply to Jerusalem.

This low-lying section of rippling hills is dangerous, as well as fatiguing. How easy it would be for a lonely traveler to fall victim to robbers who suddenly swoop out of a side valley, undeterred by the watchtowers of the Romans. This important highway to the center of Judea, however, is far from deserted. Merchants are passed carrying goods up to Jerusalem. Priests or Levites, having completed their required service at the Temple, return home along this way. Nor are the travelers only Judeans. Roman soldiers and pagan businessmen travel this major artery to the east. Even some Samaritans are met.

In the middle of this area they come to an inn located in a long valley. It is a simple building, a square with rooms on three sides of a central courtyard that is closed from the outside by a wall. After a short rest, enlivened by conversation with people who recognize their famous Rabbi, they start out on the final stretch. Soon they leave the flat valley floor and climb to an inn and fort complex which

corresponds to that at the beginning of the low-lying section. The gently rising path leading to the base of the Mount of Olives from this inn is well protected by a Rome that wants the entry to Jerusalem in its iron grip. Despite the rest stop, the cumulative tiredness from the way is still unrelieved. Many think more of the soothing comfort of a bath and clean bed than of possible danger ahead. Across the valley a few homes on the outskirts of Jeremiah's hometown, Anathoth, can be seen. How often he had pleaded with a People who would not accept a true prophet as they stumbled in darkness. Jeremiah often wept for them. Today Jesus avoids the Jerusalem which rejected that prophet. Instead, He leads the twelve straight ahead to Bethany of Judea.

Bethany

Jer. 13:15-17

John 11:17-44

JOHN 11:20-27

Villagers catch sight of them and rush down to the home of Mary and Martha with the news. Martha hurries to meet the Rabbi, but Mary seems to have lost her desire to see Him Who could have at least come earlier to comfort them. She remains at home. When Martha arrives at the ridge above Bethany, Jesus can be clearly seen as He leads the twelve toward her. They present a picture similar to the shepherds leading their flocks home along the hillsides. The good Shepherd is out in front with His twelve sheep strung out behind — tired, cautious, a bit depressed, and following slowly as if to the slaughter.

In place of joyous greetings, Martha expresses her disappointment and grief. If He had only been here, Lazarus would not have died. Nevertheless, He

When Martha arrives at the ridge above Bethany, Jesus can be clearly seen as He leads the twelve toward her.

can help. He calmly assures Martha that Lazarus will rise from the dead. Being of Pharisaic background, she affirms her belief in the resurrection of the dead. Jesus, however, corrects her. It is not a future day that is the time or place of resurrection. He Himself is the Resurrection and the Life which death can never snuff out, no matter what happens physically. Seeming to comprehend, Martha responds to His assertion by proclaiming Him the anointed one — the son of God like David and the prophet like Moses! She sees in Him the fulfillment of all the hopes of that great way which He has just surmounted.

JOHN 11:28-37

As He is greeted and surrounded by a crowd of villagers inquiring about the incident in the Temple during Hanukkah or why He delayed in coming, Martha slips away and hurries home. The house is filled with women sitting on the floor in silence staring at their bereaved friend, Mary. Occasionally they break forth in lamentation as part of the ritual for showing proper respect for death. Martha whispers to Mary that Jesus wants her. Mary goes with her to meet the One Who seemingly has so disappointed them. The mourners, not able to overhear the conversation, still follow as they have so often in the past four days. They suppose that Mary will again go to weep at the tomb, throwing dirt on her head, tearing her clothes, and sobbing beside the entrance. Instead, Mary leads the women in the opposite direction to the ridge where the crowd makes way for her as she approaches Jesus. There is no greeting. She falls at His feet in her

140

complete anguish. She expresses the same feelings as Martha. If only He had been here this never would have happened. He could have prevented death. Mary breaks down as her sobs add to the cacophony of screams and wails of the other women.

The din of this utter hopelessness is incomprehensible to Jesus. Have they not seen or heard about the *first* sign when wine flowed at Cana; or that *second* sign at the same place when the official's son was made whole; or the man at Bethzatha by the Sheep Pool who, after a *third* sign, was freed from his crippled life; or the *fourth* sign when the hungry were satisfied by the shores of the Galilean sea; not to mention how the disciples had been lifted out of the very jaws of death as a *fifth* sign was given the world by Heptapegon; or here in Jerusalem just last fall, could they not see what it means when a blind man has his eyes opened! *Six* such perfectly clear *signs of His power,* and they are still so blind! Jesus trembles with anger at their rejection of all that is so manifest. When He asks them where they have laid Lazarus, these blind ones ask *Him* to come and *see!* This is too much. Jesus weeps. The reaction of the uncomprehending crowd confirms the reason for His tears. They think that He Who brings true Life is crying for the dead Lazarus! Others even express their doubts in Him. Why could He not have done something like the last time He was in Jerusalem when He opened the eyes of a person who was born blind?

John 2:1-11

John 4:46-54
John 5:2-9
John 6:10-12

John 6:18-21
John 9:4-7

Jesus descends through the village and crosses over the slope facing it where they show Him the closed tomb. Rather than begin to mourn as they expect, Jesus directs them to take away the stone. Martha's immediate interference at this request shows further the reason for the tears in Jesus' eyes. On the ridge above she had just adorned Him with all the appropriate titles as she professed

JOHN 11:38-44

On the slope facing the village is the tomb.

141

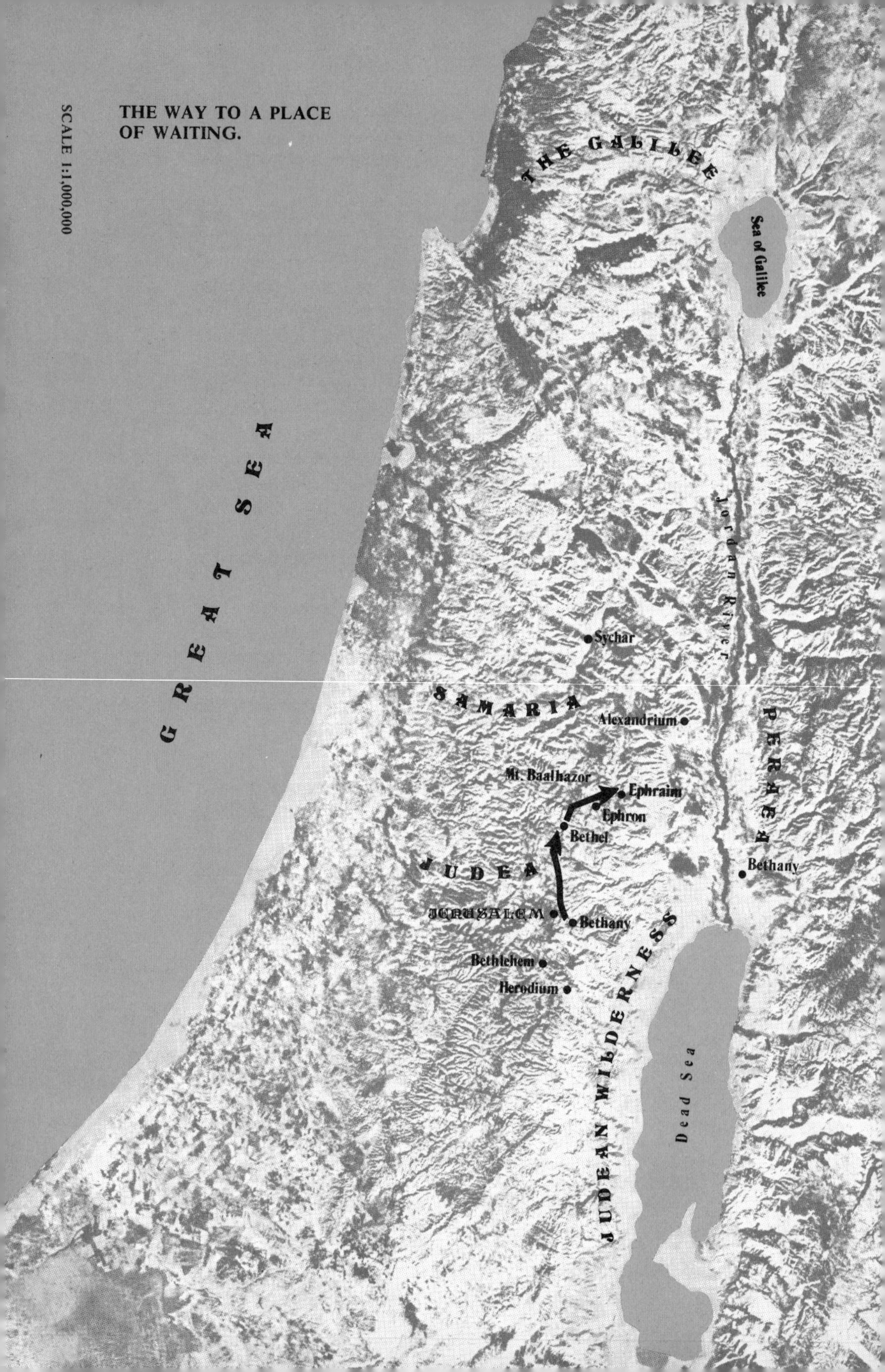

THE WAY TO A PLACE
OF WAITING.

SCALE 1:1,000,000

GREAT SEA

THE GALILEE

Sea of Galilee

Jordan River

Sychar

SAMARIA

Alexandrium

PEREA

Mt. Baalhazor

Ephraim

Ephron

Bethel

Bethany

JUDEA

JERUSALEM

Bethany

Bethlehem

Herodium

JUDEAN WILDERNESS

Dead Sea

her trust in Him. Now in the graveyard below, she cannot see past the stench of death (which must have greatly increased in the past four days).

As they work to loosen the tightly-fitting stone, Jesus lifts up His eyes and hands, and gives thanks for the Glory about to be manifest to the world. Then looking toward the black square of the opening, He shouts: "Lazarus, come out!" There is a rustling within and shocked silence without. Slowly and laboriously the bound figure struggles and works its way toward the small opening. Jesus orders the dumbfounded bystanders to release him. The beloved Lazarus emerges. The bonds of death are snapped! Life from death is the perfect sign — *the seventh.*

After the initial shock has passed, many express their faith in Jesus. Others hurry over the Mount of Olives to inform the officials of the People. As the report of the seventh sign spreads through Jerusalem like kindling fire through dry thorns, the Sanhedrin is convened on the Temple Mount. They are concerned for the beautiful structure surrounding them. As they eye the Antonia, they know only too well what this incredible sign might cause. They can see Jesus, proclaimed as a new Joshua, Moses, and David, staging a grand entry from the Mount of Olives as thousands turn out to support Him. They are not fools like the revolutionaries of the Galilee. They know that the Roman machine cannot be stopped once it is put into motion to crush its adversaries. This turn of events will serve only to drive that terrible monster on a rampage of destruction as the support for Jesus swells. The Temple, Jerusalem, and the whole nation could perish. JOHN 11:45-53

Caiaphas (the high priest this fateful year and who, as the high priest, is thought to have the gift of prophecy) explains the grounds on which Jesus can be eliminated. One man must be sacrificed for the good of the whole People. One man must be lost so that the whole nation can be saved. He does not realize how accurate are his words. In that sacrifice, not only the nation will be saved, but those of the Diaspora will be gathered into one. The council immediately resolves to put Jesus to death.

Word quickly spreads to Bethany of the impending action. In order to wait for the hour, Jesus flees Jerusalem with the twelve. He is now a condemned criminal with a price on His head. He moves directly north on the road they had taken almost two years ago on their way to Samaria. However, He does not continue north to the welcoming Samaritans when He passes Bethel. He turns northeast on a pathway seldom used except by the back villagers who, on rare occasions, go to market in the larger villages or to the feasts in Jerusalem. Avoiding Ephron just to the south, He crosses over Mount Baalhazor, leading His disciples to the safety of a small, low-lying, little-visited village by the edge of the desert — Ephraim. There will be warmth here during the cold winter months of waiting. JOHN 11:54

chapter nine

The Anointing

As the first Sabbath in April draws to a close, Jesus informs the disciples that on the coming day, the first day of the week, they will return to Jerusalem for the Passover. The remaining six days until Passover will give sufficient time to assure their purity during the feast. This period is observed by most pilgrims as a safeguard against unwittingly contacting any uncleanness. The thought of heading back to Jerusalem where death has already been decided for their Rabbi must frighten the disciples. Their reluctance to leave Ephraim increases with the dawn of the first day of the week.

Ephraim is wonderfully warm at the beginning of April. Its barley fields tucked inside the desert's edge stand tall, waiting for the harvest whose beginning will be marked by the coming Feast of Unleavened Bread. The spring of Ephraim, swollen by heavy winter rains that have drenched the highlands of northern Judea, explodes in a torrential cannonade of water. The resulting stream winds through the fields on its way to water the palm groves around Archelaus. Even the rocky slopes where the valley nestles have come alive with the red, white, and yellow desert flowers that seem to grow miraculously from stone. As Jesus and the twelve mount the steep path (the demanding start of their long 22-mile way to Bethany), the predawn light wakens this sanctuary's songbirds, and beckons flocks of doves from their niches high on the cliff-face above the spring. Goats herded from their overnight lodging above the same sheer cliff start their incredible descent to the water, seeming to delight in vertical falls that are gracefully halted by nimble feet. Shepherds who have staked out springtime desert around Ephraim as their domain, begin to lead out their flocks. Bells fastened around the necks of the head sheep and goats set up a delicate tinkling reechoed up and down the sides of the valley. Songbirds add a descant to this pastoral bell chorus as the steady, periodic shouts of the shepherds provide the percussion's rhythm. The valley is difficult to leave.

The way to the highlands follows a tortuous series of switchbacks along which the disciples must climb to 340 times their own height. When they reach the curve from which they view the valley for the last time, they see Bethany of Peraea in the distance. How different was spring two years ago when Nathanael there proclaimed the Master King of Israel. Leaving Ephraim and passing *John 1:49* through the tribe of the same name, this King seems as broken and forlorn as the Israel that once claimed these hills. Their way is far from the easy trip to Cana of *John 1:35-2:11* the Galilee they made with Him two years ago! That sojourn ended in the warm welcome of a halcyon Galilean spring. This week begins as an upward struggle. →

When the band rounds the last switchback of the climb, they have their last *Left:* opportunity to look at the North. Memories are warm. Deceptively close are the *Ephraim*

The Caesarea
where Pilate
resides.
John 4:39-42
proud Mounts Gerizim and Ebal. The cut between them in which Sychar-Shechem lies is clearly visible. There Jesus was proclaimed Savior of the world. The fortress of the Alexandrium watching over the Jordan Valley at their feet attests that Caesar is still king of the world. In the clearness of a spring morning, the Galilee is brought miraculously near, as far off the faint outline of mighty snow-frosted Mount Hermon can be seen. In the North, crowds had tried to John 6:15 proclaim Jesus King; here in Judea the result of His rejection of their effort is evident. They turn to complete the remaining short climb to the top of Mount 2 Sam. 13:1-39 Baalhazor. This lofty landmark reinforces thoughts of broken and rejected kingship. Absalom murdered his half brother here following the rape of his sister, Tamar. This was symptomatic of the unstable beginning of the royal family. It ended in Absalom's bid to dethrone his father David.

As they cross Baalhazor, the way to the Mount of Olives and Bethany confronts them. Weary already from the demanding climb with still a long-day's journey toward uncertainty, there is no rejoicing. Although the Mount of Olives and Bethany lie below Mount Baalhazor, the way which is hacked apart by several deep valleys represent just another, more prolonged climb. Although the highway to Jerusalem along the ridge is easier and faster, Jesus must keep to this difficult path. The ridge road is too well controlled and could possibly lead to captivity before the *hour*. The highway is left for the procurator.

That representative of Caesar, Pilate, is preparing to visit Jerusalem for Passover. With hundreds of pilgrims coming from every corner of the country

and distant lands as well, Rome must be on guard in case of insurrection. Pilate's permanent residence is not in the Judean capital. He oversees both Judea and Samaria from the city bearing his lord's name, Caesarea. Because there are so many cities honoring that great purveyor of "peace" to the world, the Caesarea where Pilate resides is surnamed "Maritima" because of its location by the Great Sea. It is difficult to leave such a gem of a Roman city. All the comforts of Rome are here, including a stadium, theater, baths, and fine shops. The elegant buildings are constructed or faced not by the ugly brown sandstone of the coast, but by the finest of limestone. This was transported from the Judean hills to give the city a special white gleam, accented by the deep blue of the sea before it.

At Antipatris water gushes out, forming a river appropriately called Waters of Pegae, Springs.

Herod the Great had employed the most advanced western technology in constructing this port of entry to the east. Although this part of the coast has no natural harbor, Herod created one by dropping stones measuring up to 50 feet in length into over 120 feet of water. The resulting breakwater allows this majestic port to extend far out into the sea. In remembrance of his master, Herod named this work, Sebastios. In fact, the city is crowned with a temple which houses a colossal statue of Caesar. It looks over the harbor area, welcoming those who enter the land.

Josephus, War I, 408-415

Pilate travels to Jerusalem under the protective eye of the Tenth Legion's cavalry. He rides in a luxurious coach cushioned to make the way a bit smoother. The well-constructed highway is yet another credit to western technology, having been built through a worthless swamp called the Plain of Sharon, *Levelness.*

147

Thick with impassable scrub oaks and filled with lagoons of stagnant water, travel through it is almost impossible except by this excellent Roman highway.

Pilate rests for the night at Antipatris located at the end of the *Levelness* and the entrance way into the hill country. Water collected on this side of the Judean range gushes out at this city, forming one of the larger rivers of the country — appropriately called the Waters of Pegae, *Springs*. This well-watered land contrasts with the barren hills through which the party of Pilate climbs the following day.

Pilate's convoy is not alone. The last of the pilgrim bands from abroad land at Caesarea and hurry to reach Jerusalem in time to prepare for the feast. Some are on foot. Others who have gained from the wealth of Rome ride their horses or, like Pilate, travel in carriages. Their native tongue is Greek or Latin. Aramaic JOHN 11:52 sounds as foreign to them as it does to Pilate. These children of God who have been scattered abroad in the Diaspora return to their spiritual homeland as foreigners.

They look to former Ramathaim (now called Arimathea) on the ridge north 1 Sam. 9:1-10:1 of the highway and recall the first king, Saul. There in Samuel's hometown was born the hope that a king of God's People would one day rule the nations. In complete privacy, Samuel had poured a jar of anointing oil on Saul's head and kissed his face as a sign that his enthronement as prince of the People would follow. That newly-anointed farmer walked home to Gibeah along the very highway Caesar's representative now travels in regal splendor.

Pilgrims, soldiers, and Pilate rest at the large village of Timnath-serah halfway to the ridge of the Judean highlands. This is the hometown of the great Josh. 24:29-30 Joshua-Jesus who had freed the land from pagan domination. He chose this village (strategically placed for guarding the entrance to the highlands) as his inheritance. Pilgrims visit Joshua's tomb by the village. Leaving Timnath-serah Josh. 24:33 behind, the tombs of Eleazar and Phineas soon appear across a valley at Gibeah of Ephraim. Their descendants will perform the priestly office when the Passover lamb is slaughtered this week as they pray for another Joshua-Jesus who will cast out the ruler of the world.

Having passed through the first valley below Mount Baalhazor, the disciples pause to rest at the village of Ephron. They have a fine view of the highway leading south from Samaria to join the road from Caesarea. Its smooth sweep passes Gibeah of Saul and crosses Mount Scopus to transport the world to Jerusalem. The highway runs parallel to the rough, valley-hacked path they will follow. This back way, bereft of the lifeblood of the empire, is lonely and deserted except for a few farmers on their way to the fields or shepherds returning from pasturing their flocks in the desert. This route, however, is not Is. 10:27-32 unknown. It once served the Assyrian army which conquered the villages along this way as it moved to Nob on the Mount of Olives. There the Assyrian host shook its mighty fist at a cowering Jerusalem.

The small band that moves from Ephron to Rimmon has no fist to shake. They possess no great power like Assyria's which can bring a misguided Is. 11:1-10 Jerusalem to its knees. They are an insignificant band following a Jesus from *Sprout*. After the Assyrian punishment, Isaiah had promised a shoot of Jesse Overleaf:
Michmash who would be a sign to the nations. To be sure, this Jesus possesses the wisdom,

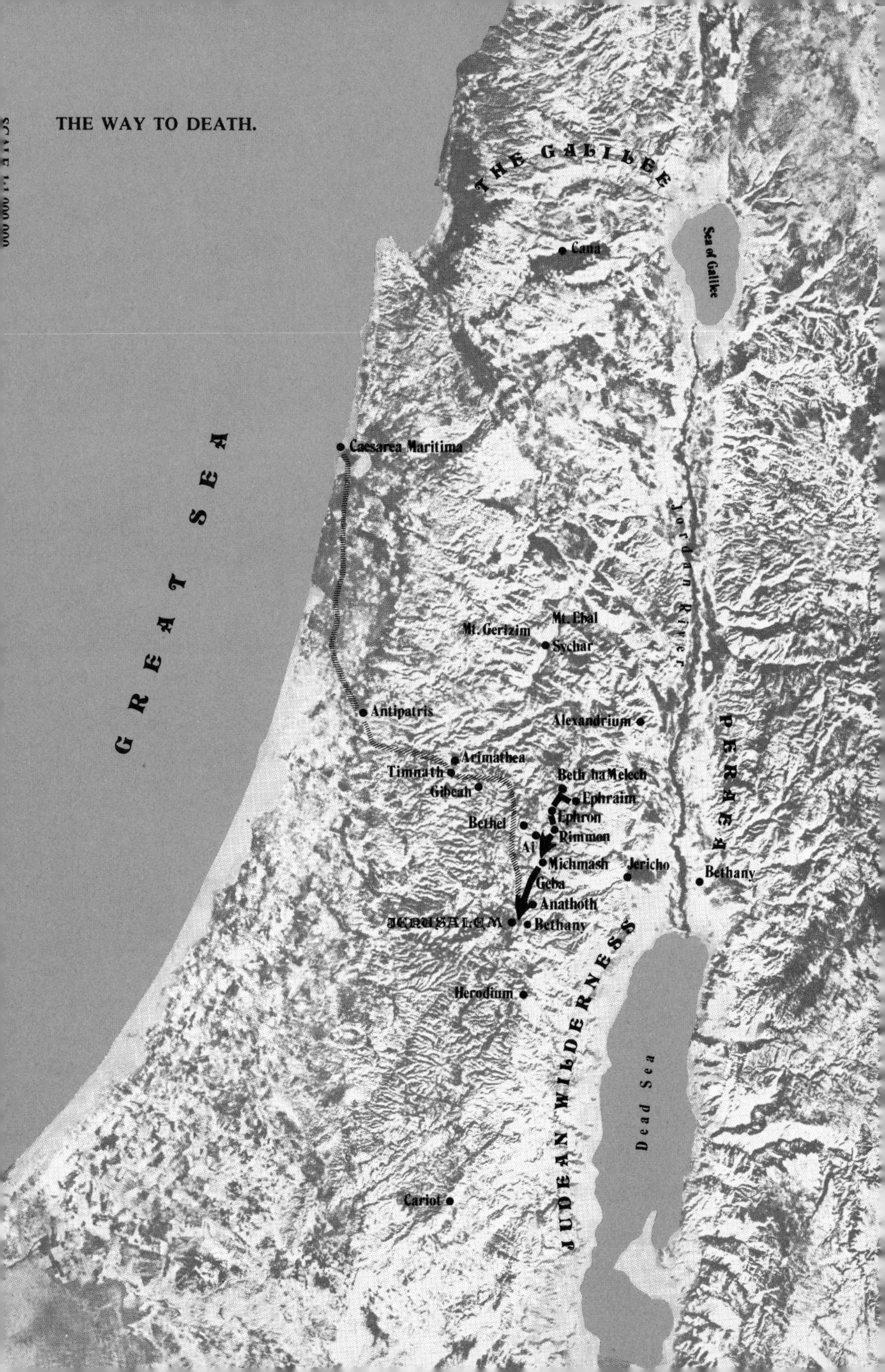

THE WAY TO DEATH.

SCALE 1:1,000,000

THE GALILEE

Sea of Galilee

Cana

GREAT SEA

Caesarea Maritima

Jordan River

Mt. Ebal
Mt. Gerizim
Sychar

Antipatris

Alexandrium

PERAEA

Arimathea
Timnath
Gibeah
Beth haMelech
Ephraim
Ephron
Rimmon
Bethel
Ai
Michmash
Jericho
Geba
Bethany
Anathoth
JERUSALEM
Bethany

Herodium

JUDEAN WILDERNESS

Dead Sea

Cariot

understanding, counsel, knowledge, and fear of the Lord which Isaiah spoke about — but where is His might as they head to Bethany on this back road?

Forty minutes later they round the base of the hill on which Rimmon stands. They see its namesake, *Pomegranate,* necklaced about the village in red-blossomed finery. Rimmon symbolizes Isaiah's hope of life. Once the tribes all but annihilated Benjamin in a terrible battle that raged over the hills in front of the twelve. A small remnant of that tribe survived because they found refuge here by the desert's edge. As the disciples look across the bloodied territory of Benjamin (which they will cross on the way to Bethany) they realize that there still is no end to the attempt of brother to eliminate brother. Jerusalem is also part of Benjamin.

Judg. 20:29-48

Judg. 1:21

In the valley through which they now pass, Joshua had once dared to bring a small force to draw the pagans away from their huge city, Ai. With the army of the People of God encamped on the Rimmon side of this valley and an ambush waiting behind Ai on the other side, Joshua feigned flight, only to turn on the unsuspecting pagan forces who had been drawn into his trap. Ai was left the pile of ruins it remains to this day — a testimony to the power and leadership of that great conqueror whose name their Rabbi bears. The king of Ai had been hung by the gate of the city, a sign of God's triumph over the forces of evil. That triumph seems reversed as this Jesus reaches the other side of the deep valley, and ominous Jerusalem again comes into view.

Josh. 8:1-28

An hour and a half after leaving Rimmon, they approach Michmash. The villagers stare at this odd, tired-looking band that slowly trudges the main street. Obviously, from the accent of their Aramaic greetings, most come from the Galilee. Obviously, too, they are headed up to Jerusalem for Passover festivities. Why do they go this way? Galilean pilgrims pass through the Jordan Valley going up the Jericho Road. It is not difficult to conclude that this could be part of the resistance.

At the edge of the village a deep pass lies before them. The way is anything but inviting. The steep side facing them is most forbidding. The beginning of the pass can be seen as it drops down from the ridge highway where Rome moves with ease. From there they control all entry into Jerusalem. The band has no other alternative than to plunge into this deep line of divison between North and South. This was once the center of a battle between Saul and the Philistines.

The Philistines had massed their frightening might at Michmash. Saul's small army facing them across the pass had none of the fine weaponry these masters of the coastal plain possessed. They lacked the technical skill needed to produce iron. Their last stand seemed hopeless. As the disciples face the wilderness during their midday pause in the center of the pass, the vertical cliffs of Bozez and Seneh rise before them. Jonathan, alone except for his armor bearer, had challenged the Philistines there by daring to scale the cliff to the enemy's camp. The Philistines were so surprised that they fled, causing panic throughout the huge encampment. As the disciples continue on their way out of the valley, that victory of a few against incalculable forces gives some encouragement.

1 Sam. 13:5-23

Geba, *Hill,* (which appears when they reach the top) marked the northern boundary of Judah at the time of the divided kingdom. One day the valley which

Zech. 14:9-11

they descend after Geba and Mount Scopus which they must then ascend, will be turned into a plain. Jerusalem will then stand above the land as God, the King, enters to reign over a city cleansed of pagan domination. Their sore legs stress how far away that day must be!

As they begin the demanding climb out of the valley, Gibeah of Saul rises before them. Gibeah's lofty setting does not correspond to the tragedy that was played out there. The reign of the first king of God's People was spoiled by the moves and countermoves for power between Saul and the young upstart, David. Ramah, which is not far from Gibeah, recalls Judah's final experience with kings. When Jerusalem fell and Judah was taken captive, Ramah became the detention center before the leaders of the People were taken into exile. The hope of the return of the children of God scattered abroad began there.

Jer. 40:1-12

After passing through one last dip made triply deep by the long-day's journey, Anathoth comes into view. This is the hometown of Ramah's most famous prisoner, Jeremiah. He pleaded with the People in Jerusalem to again follow the ancient path, the good way. They refused. How often he had returned to this quiet village by the desert's edge to lick his wounds, only somehow to find himself forced to return again to that city of wrong. The Rabbi in front of the twelve, silently lifting His body up that way with firm, determined steps, burns with that same prophetic resolve.

Jer. 16:16
Jer. 20:7-18

The top of Mount Scopus is reached by an aching, sweating group to whom the cooler midafternoon air gives no comfort. There is no uplifting joy when they see the Temple — only the sobering realization that there is no turning back. Jesus and the twelve move along the ridge, passing the imperceptible boundary between Mount Scopus and the Mount of Olives. When Jesus reaches Bethphage at the end of the ridge, He does not descend to Jerusalem. Instead, He goes through the village and down the back side of the Mount of Olives toward Bethany. The sight of the majestic Herodium by Bethlehem recalls the hope of many that at this feast there will again arise one who will be anointed, crowned, and enthroned as king of the Judeans.

While a delicious meal is quickly prepared at the home of Mary, Martha, and Lazarus, basins are brought for bathing. After Jesus and His disciples soak their feet, the sisters give them olive oil to further soothe the sting of the way. Completely refreshed and revived, they are ready for supper as the evening of the second day of the week begins.

JOHN 12:2-8

A perfume jar

When the meal (which Martha serves) is nearly finished, Mary kneels beside Jesus, letting down her long hair. The disciples are chagrined! Women do not do this in public. They are further suprised as the Rabbi allows her to take His feet in her hand. She has a large, finely-fashioned perfume jar which must hold at least twelve ounces. As she pours the precious liquid over His feet, the well known fragrance permeates the room, as does her love for Him. The guests blink in disbelief. Twelve ounces of nard (an expensive perfume from northern India) must cost at least 300 denari. It is almost a year's wages for a common laborer that she throws away in an instant! Nor does that end the shock. She humiliates herself as she wipes and rubs the perfumed feet with her black silken hair. Not even a lowly slave would do such a thing.

The spokesman for the group, respected for his counsel and entrusted with their money, Judas from Cariot, articulates well many of their own thoughts. How could Jesus permit such a thing? Think how the money gained by selling this nard could have helped the poor! (As they nod their approval, the disciples have no idea that Judas has betrayed their trust by embezzling.) Jesus' response, "Let her alone, should she keep it for the day of My burial?" is difficult to understand. Certainly they did not come to Bethany, the place of resurrection, for the Master's funeral! Now is the time for the royal anointing — not on Jesus' feet but His head — not in such a degrading way by a woman, but by the male leadership of the People.

On the morning of the second day of the week, they rest from the demanding journey. Bethany slowly fills with curious pilgrims who have heard reports of the raising of a dead man. Their verification of this sign quickly builds enthusiastic support for Jesus as the officials of Jerusalem look on in horror. This JOHN 12:9-46 36 will surely be brought to the attention of Pilate! Jesus must be eliminated quickly, and Lazarus too, before disaster overtakes the nation. How to prevent the coronation of this Rabbi is the urgent question. It is impossible to arrest Him openly in Bethany. That could spark a riot which, in turn, would touch off a deadly confrontation with law-and-order-conscious Rome.

By midafternoon the excitement of the crowd is beyond containment. Jesus, for once, does not dampen their enthusiasm. He even seems to encourage it. With the disciples acting as the bodyguards of their Anointed One, He leaves Bethany. Surprisingly, He starts the steep climb up the backside of the Mount of Olives on the way to Jerusalem. The hopes of the crowd soar. This is the moment for which the disciples have waited. He will enter Jerusalem in defiance of the threat of death leveled by the leaders of the Pharisees and the pro-Roman priesthood. The *People* rally at this hour of glory! Galileans are out in full force, supported by Judeans from outside Jerusalem who, as the Galileans, are staying on this side of the Mount of Olives. They had been idling away their time during the week of waiting before the sacrifice and now are caught up in the moment of triumph. One feels the Mount of Olives is almost ready to split open as the Holy One of God and Savior of the world goes to Jerusalem in triumph. Rome is about to be crushed! Patrolling soldiers, surprised by this fast-building tidal wave, retreat, letting it wash past as it picks up young and old in its wake. Bethphage is reached with a breathlessness caused not so much from the climb, as from charged and tensed nerves.

154

News of the approaching Joshua-Jesus reaches the city. Racing out to be part of the grand entry, a responding crowd rushes up the Mount of Olives. This seems to be the climax of all the great feasts of the People as Passover and Succoth join in the beginning and ending of the *year* of the Lord. This is the answer to the Succoth prayer for the coming of the great king who assures, once and for all, a Passover of joy as the People are liberated from all tyranny and returned to paradise. Filled with assurance, they grab for palm branches, nearly stripping the few trees growing in the Kidron Valley and in private gardens. As the People waving lulabim meet Him near the top of the mount, the air suddenly explodes with shouts of Hosanna! Hosanna!! Hosanna!!! The assertion of lone Nathanael in the beginning now becomes the mighty chorus of Jerusalem, the Galilee, Judea, and the Diaspora...

News of the approaching Joshua-Jesus reaches the city.

John 1:49

> Blessed is He who comes in the name of the
> Lord even the *KING OF ISRAEL!* Hosanna!!

JOHN 12:12-14

Jesus, swamped by the surging mass but in full control, grabs a frightened donkey's colt tethered by the wayside. He sits on it to be above the adoring crowd that presses around Him ready for the final, long-awaited grand entry. The dreams of Zechariah and Zephaniah are fulfilled before the crowd.

Zech. 9:9
Zeph. 3:16

> Fear not, daughter of Zion,
> behold your king is coming,
> *sitting* on a donkey's colt!

Pharisaic and priestly leaders nervously watch from the Temple area, waiting for the climactic entry of this hastily declared king. They eye an equally nervous Antonia tightening its muscles for the inevitable clash when the crowds reach the Holy Place. Troops are put on alert. Swords are drawn. It is impossible for the leaders of the People to stop the parade now. The entire world, it seems, has swarmed out to bring Him to the Temple in triumph in spite of Caesar's might.

Greek-speaking People of God who have arrived from the Diaspora by way of Caesarea underscore the truth of the leaders concern. These representatives of the world want to see Jesus. Working their way through the crowd, they single out the disciple with a Greek name, Philip. Accompanied by Andrew, Philip conveys their request to Jesus Who addresses not only these representatives of the Diaspora, but everyone else as well. As He begins to speak, the crowd suddenly hushes with an explosive silence of anticipation. They strain for His last words of encouragement before they escort Him to the Temple for the beginning

of His reign. His first words raise their expectations to a feverish pitch as He declares that now is the time for the Son of Man to be glorified. To be sure, as He begins to talk about "seeds," excitement is checked for an instant, and pleading expressions on the disciples' faces cry out for Him not to lose this triumphant moment with holy talk!

> Indeed I tell you, unless a grain of wheat
> falls into the ground and dies, it remains
> alone, but if it dies it bears much fruit.

As He continues to clarify His remarks their hopes soar again. Now He sounds like the perfect commander, preparing his troops for the challenging battle ahead. They look down to the forboding Antonia and the Roman troops forming by its side. In a moment the clash must take place:

> He who loves his life loses it, and
> he who hates his life in this world
> will keep it for eternal life.
> If anyone serves Me, he must follow Me,
> and where I am, there shall My servant be also.
> If anyone serves Me, the Father will honor him.

The speech is perfect after all, and voices are ready to give the battle cry as they triumphantly move with Him against the evil powers of the world. Yet, the young donkey still is not spurred on. With some impatience growing in the crowd, He continues to speak of being troubled, praying as if to gain courage for the battle He must lead. He will not ask the Father to stop this moment for *the hour has come.* Suddenly there is a clap of thunder that fills the crowd with the desire to enter the cosmic battle for which this surely is the signal. Others even whisper that an angel has spoken to Him declaring in the thunderous voice, "I have glorified Your name and I will glorify it again." Jesus shouts that this was to inform them that this is the final *hour*. The ruler of the world shall be cast out! With smiles bursting, cheers rising, and palm branches waving defiantly in the face of the Antonia, the crowd is ready.

Jesus still does not move the donkey. He speaks of being *lifted up* from the earth and bringing all people to Himself. Some in the crowd shout out their astonishment as their impatience to be on the way grows. The anointed one is to stay forever. What does He mean by being *lifted up?* As the sun begins to sink into the world, Jesus looks over the sea of faces about Him which are already being caught in the coming night's shadows and warns:

JOHN 12:32-36

> The Light is with you for a little longer.
> Walk while you have the Light, lest the darkness overtake you;
> he who walks in the darkness does not know where he goes.
> While you have the Light, believe in the Light
> that you may become sons of Light.

Then He slides off the donkey and quickly loses Himself in the darkness. The parade is over. The stunned crowd, after standing in uncomprehending silence begins to disperse — grumbling, complaining, disillusioned. Their shattered hopes leave them bitter and feeling like fools. He is certainly no David! Roman officials below, seeing the crowd scatter as suddenly as it gathered, are puzzled but relieved. The sun sets. Night comes....

chapter ten

The Meeting of the Forces

As the sixth day of the week begins, Jerusalem is filled to overflowing with pilgrims. The normally crowded city has swollen from its usual 25,000 inhabitants to almost 100,000. Fortunate pilgrims have found lodging in the city, but many have been forced to go to nearby villages. Others camp under the stars even during these often chilly nights of early April. However, all must eat the Passover meal within the city limits of Jerusalem which for this occasion extends beyond the city walls. The twelve have been informed that Jesus wishes to dine with them at a home in the city this evening, which begins the day before — Passover.

They enter the sparsely furnished dining area as the day's last light fades. Small lamps set about the room on stands or in nooks and along the low, narrow table in the middle of the room, give a muted glow that conveys a sad feeling of endings. There is to be a special meal, for cushions have been spread around the table. The disciples do not sit to eat as usual, but rather recline. This custom is unusual, for it is the style of Roman banquets. However, on all special occasions, as tomorrow evening at Passover, this manner of eating is observed by rich or poor alike. This is to remind them that one day God will liberate them so that they may take the place of the occupying pagans. They lie on their left sides, supporting themselves with their left hands. Their right hands are free to take the food which the women now serve from the far end of the table. Peter is at this end of the table, always ready to go out and get things better organized or protect the Master from intrusions. The others have arranged themselves along the sides of the table with Jesus at the head. On His right side lies the beloved John. The place of honor to Jesus' left goes to the treasurer of the group, their trusted counselor and spokesman, Judas.

While they are finishing the meal, Jesus stands, *lays down* His clothes, and wraps a long, narrow linen cloth about His loins. He allows one end of the cloth to hang down from His waist and serve as a towel. He thus becomes a lowly servant. Taking a pitcher of water and a small basin, He begins to bathe the feet of the twelve. Of course they are clean. They took a bath before coming to dinner and washed their dusty feet again before entering the room. Obviously Jesus intends His actions to be symbolic, reminding one of Jeremiah's method of teaching in this city. Nevertheless, symbol or no symbol, Peter, who is embarrassed by the Rabbi acting like a slave, absolutely refuses to go along. How could he possibly let the One Whom he loves and respects above all others

JOHN 13:1

JOHN 13:2-11

Left:
The way to the High Priest's residence.

perform such a menial task for him? He would gladly play the role of slave for the Master. Jesus brushes aside his protestations. If Peter will not allow Him to be his servant, then he is no disciple. Peter, his wonderfully impetuous self, immediately demands that Jesus give him a complete bath! The Rabbi must remind him that it is not the action itself that is important, but rather what it symbolizes. They are all clean, except one who will not truly be cleansed. He is the one like David's trusted counselor, Ahithophel, who betrayed the great king. How aptly David described this betrayal as Ahithophel's lifting his heel against him. In the East when someone turns a heel to another this signifies the desire to transfer filth and a curse to the despised one. So Jesus' betrayer will do this night.

JOHN 13:12-20

2 Sam. 15:31

Ps. 41:9

Returning to the head of the table, their Shepherd *takes up* His clothing — almost as if He is acting out His previous claim to *lay down* His life for His sheep so that later He might *take it up* again. Jesus asks that they continue to wash the feet of others. They who honor Him with titles like Rabbi and Mar, *Teacher and Master,* have had their feet washed by Him. Therefore, they should do this act of love for each other.

John 10:11-18

As evening progresses, Jesus speaks of one who will betray Him. Peter, always having one ear tuned to the Rabbi, nods to John, motioning for him to ask who it is. In a world where men show much affection for each other, the beloved John is lying against the breast of the Rabbi. Jesus occasionally dips a piece of bread into the dish in front of them, scooping up the last remnants of the meal which He places in the beloved's mouth. To feed another is a supreme sign of love. Other close friends among the disciples occasionally do the same. In this way, lying close to Jesus, John leans back and quietly asks to whom He is referring. Jesus replies that it is the one to whom He will give a morsel of bread. Breaking off a piece of bread, He dips it into the dish before Him. Turning to the place of honor on His left, He tenderly places it in the mouth of Judas.

JOHN 13:21-30

The One Who bears all forgiveness chooses for His last communication with His betrayer not harsh words of reproach, but rather this sign of love. The recipient is like another Satan. Satan was once the trusted counselor of God, respected and praised by the hosts of heaven. One day, however, he turned against God and was driven out of the heavenly company. Jesus' only word to the one in whom Satan has entered is to do what he must do quickly. No one, including John, has any idea of what is happening because their expectations are too rigid. They think they know the highly honored Judas perfectly. When he leaves they suppose it is to make arrangements for the Passover sacrifice, or to provide for the poor. Judas disappears into the night.

Enoch 86:1-87:4

Jesus now announces that He will be with them only a little longer. Peter, always first to speak his mind, asks where He intends to go. When Jesus replies that he cannot follow Him to that place, Peter proclaims that he is ready to lay down his life for Him. Again Jesus will not let his rashness run away with him. He informs the brave Peter that he will betray Him three times before the cock crows this very night.

JOHN 13:31-38

Jesus continues, explaining that He is leaving to prepare a place for them. Thomas, who had pointed out the foolishness of the way to Bethany and yet was always right behind the Master, still wants to follow the way of Jesus — or at least to know the place where He is going so he can follow. Summing up all the

JOHN 14:1-7

hours they have spent with Him — covering the territory from Judea to the Galilee and back again, calling to memory the heavy moments of deep thought, broken and lifted by the laughter and jokes along the paths, pointing to all that He has revealed to them about Himself during those long hours together along the way — Jesus answers that He is the *WAY* along which the Truth will be known so that Life might truly be theirs.

Philip also does not understand, although he was one of the first to receive a call, following all the way from Bethany of Peraea. He pleads with Jesus to let them see the Father. Jesus asserts that what he has seen, touched, and heard during the days and months along the way has been the revelation of the Father Who is in Him.

JOHN 14:8-14

Judas, another disciple by the same name as the satanic citizen of Cariot, grows impatient with Jesus only manifesting Himself to them. When will He reveal His might to the world? Jesus answers that the Spirit which guides to Peace will only be given to His followers, not the world. His gift of peace is not another Pax Romana, the much heralded "peace" of the world brought by a "golden age" ushered in by Caesar Augustus. It is not the ephemeral "peace" which the great king of the Judeans, Herod, strove to enforce in this land and the Herodians still seek as they build up Sebastia, Tiberias, or the Caesareas. His Peace is completely different from what the world has to offer. Now is the time for that other Peace to be bestowed as He goes to the Father.

JOHN 14:15-31

After the wine of blessing has been passed to conclude the meal, they prepare to leave. Jesus lingers a little longer. As the sweet wine warms their hearts, Jesus explains that He is the True Vine. The disciples spreading out from Him around the table are the branches. His words carry thoughts to the hills of Judea now covered with newly budding vines and raise the hopes these vineyards silently express. The vine is Judah's life, as Jacob underscored in his blessing. The poor, dry, rocky hills south of Jerusalem can support the sturdy vine which provides many of the essentials for the People's life.

JOHN 15:1-17

Gen. 49:10-12

The tender leaves of spring make excellent salads or fine greens in which to wrap meat for cooking. The sucker branches which stunt the development of the clusters will not be thrown away when the vines are *cleansed* of them in early summer. In this wood-poor land, they are gathered and stacked to provide valuable tinder.

The fruit of late summer and early fall will be pressed into the fine wines that give spirit to high and holy occasions. They also strengthen the sick. Some of the wine will be allowed to become vinegar for spicing meals or cleaning wounds. The grapes themselves, from the early sour fruit that sets teeth on edge to the doubly sweet overripe fruit at the season's end, will provide fine desserts. Some of the clusters will be dried under the strong September sun to produce raisins for the barren months of winter when fruit disappears from the land. The thick syrup extracted from the grapes will provide sugar for daily use in beverages and cooking. This is called debash, the *honey* that flows in the Promised Land.

Ex. 3:8

In fall, when the final fruit is gleaned, the remaining leaves will also be used. The greener ones will become feed for donkeys and goats when the dried stubble on the hillsides can no longer support them, while the yellowing leaves will be

Jesus is the true vine; His disciples are the branches.

plowed into the soil to further nourish the vine. When the barren branches are cut from the vine in the dead of winter (sacrificed in order to make the vine stronger when new life-bearing branches sprout in their places) they, too, will be put to use. From them will come the material for weaving baskets in a dry land where reeds seldom grow. The branches of last year will carry this year's fruit to the world. Dried and used for fires, they will provide warmth in winter. Nor is the sturdy and thick vine itself ever simply discarded. Supports for roofs, firewood, and even handles come from it. When alive, the vine is lifted up so that its branches may cover porches under whose shade people can revive themselves.

Micah 4:4

To sit at peace with one's neighbor under the vine is the dream of paradise this Passover. Life was like this in the golden days of Solomon. The prophets promise

1 Kings 4:25

that paradise will return when those who would destroy the vine of God are vanquished.

Ps. 80:8-19

It is little wonder that the image of the vine was chosen to describe not only Judah, but all of God's People. The psalmist well describes the wandering that followed the first Passover as God's bringing of the true vine to the Promised Land. At first it prospered, but gradually was broken and finally burned as the People allowed other vinedressers to enter God's vineyard. The People pray that this Passover God will again turn to His Vine — a Son whom He will rear for Himself so that through that Remnant His vineyard might be planted again. This

162

hope is even depicted above the door of the Sanctuary. A golden grapevine is hung above it which is constantly made more fruitful by offerings of huge metallic clusters of golden grapes.

The vine is Judah's Life.

Josephus,War V, 210

John 2:19-21

John 2:1-11

John 6:53-56

Jesus, Who two Passovers ago asserted that He was Himself the Temple, now proclaims that He is the True Vine, the true Remnant of Israel and Judah. His first sign at Cana showed He was the true Giver of Wine. He now explains to the disciples that in the days following that sign they have been *cleansed,* pruned of all that would spoil the good fruit of their life in Him. They who have just drunk the fruit of the vine, blessed and poured out by Him, will remain one with Him. They, the branches, and He, the Vine, have become One. Apart from His sustaining stem and root there can be no true building and weaving material, drink, food, or sweetening in the world. The useless branches that bear no fruit will be cut off in the pruning of autumn and burned in the judging fire. Those bearing fruit will know the strength of the supported branch, the new life of the shade, and the joy of the wine. That Oneness in the Vine is true love which the world can never take away.

Leaving the cozy warmth of low burning lamps, Jesus and His followers enter into the cold night. The white limestone houses crowding the hill sloping to the Tyropoeon Valley take on a skeletal appearance under a moon which will be completely full for the Passover feast tomorrow evening. As the wind whips up

JOHN 18:1 — 27

the street of stairs which leads down to the city gate by the Kidron Valley, they bundle their mantles tightly about themselves. Jerusalem's changeable desert clime is felt. Warm days can turn to bone chilling nights.

2 Sam. 15:13-15, 16:14

After Jesus leaves the city, He *goes forth* over the dry Kidron Valley which flows with water only in the winter months. They pass beneath the ancient City of David as they start up the valley along the way David fled when betrayed by Absalom. David *went forth* along this way to escape death at the hands of his own son. Unlike David, Jesus does not run away from the threat of death behind Him when He reaches the other side of the Kidron. He turns from the way that would lead to safety beyond the Jordan River and enters a garden grove of olive trees. The spot is familiar to the disciples, for it is Jesus' favorite place for prayer and quiet meditation in the night. Here they have been always alone.

They sit under the trees and gaze across to Jerusalem rising on the other side of the Kidron Valley. The city looms ominously in the moonlight, the outlines of its buildings stark and foreboding. In front of them the top of the Sanctuary is silhouetted against the skyline. Its brilliance has muted to a shadow of itself. The Antonia rises beside it like a hill which casts a further shadow across the Temple. Its light-filled windows give the impression of a raging fire within. There is much activity tonight as patrols come and go to keep a tight rein on the Passover crowd.

The city south of the Holy Place is terribly still. Weak lamplight is snuffed out in an odd window here and there. But in contrast to the darkness of the houses and palaces, there is bright light in the courts of the high priest's compound at the top of the Upper City. They are probably checking on last-minute details in preparation for tomorrow's sacrifice. In comparison, the long outline of the procurator's residence next door is rather subdued. Pilate is resting.

JOHN 18:2-3

Judas, meanwhile, has reported to the Antonia as prearranged with the authorities. They have taken every precaution that Jesus' arrest will be swift and decisive. Without explaining their full intentions, they have negotiated with Pilate to use his forces to assure their goals. Pilate, anxious to avoid any trouble this Passover and more than willing to remove a potential upstart from the volatile atmosphere of Passover, gladly agreed to send a force of two hundred to back up the Temple police. This mini-army is led by a Roman centurion. Judas, knowing the place where Jesus will be alone with His small band, serves as guide. The Romans leave the Antonia armed with swords and the Temple police carry clubs. Both groups carry lanterns and torches to illuminate Jesus' place of prayer.

The disciples notice a large movement of troops leaving the dark hulk of the Antonia, slowly making its way toward the Mount of Olives. They watch more because of the beautiful procession of bobbing lights than out of concern. This is probably just another patrol to assure Roman peace. However, as the line of lights arrives at the way up the Mount of Olives, it methodically turns. The frightening clanging of swords beating against armor, and the rhythmic pounding of war sandals on the hard-packed ground grows steadily louder. As the disciples pull back in fright, Jesus moves out to confront the menacing force which grinds to a halt with the yelling of orders echoing back through the ranks.

Right: He enters a garden grove of olive trees.

164

Jesus stands tall in the murky darkness enveloping His beleaguered little band. His mantle flapping in the night breezes, He faces with commanding authority a flame-lit wall of drawn swords, clenched clubs, buckled-down iron helmets, tightly fitting breastplates, and shin guards. Then the eleven notice something that shocks them more than this display of military muscle. Half-hidden behind this band of warriors lurks their trusted treasurer — Judas!

JOHN 18:4-9

The uneasy silence is finally broken by Jesus. He must *ask them,* "whom do you seek?" An officer calls out the name and residence of the accused, "Jesus, the citizen of Nazareth." His simple reply, "I am He," is uttered with such inner control, power, and authority that it causes the pagans to pull back and the pious Judeans to bow to the ground. It is as if He has pronounced the Holy Name of God which no man dares utter. For a moment it seems as if they are bowing at His feet. In absolute control, He presses the question again, almost as if chiding this hesitant force. Again the accused One's name is intoned. He then commands

JOHN 18:10-11

them to leave His followers alone and take only Him. Peter then makes a feeble effort to defend the Undefendable. In a pathetic attempt to show his intention of carrying on the great revolt, Peter pulls a short sword concealed in his robe and strikes. However, he does not choose one of the tough, armor-clad warriors who confronts him, but a slave of the high priest, a Nabatean named Malchus, who has his back turned to Peter. He who was going to fight the enemies of Jesus to the death can manage only to nip off a slave's right earlobe, and from behind at

JOHN 18:12-14

that! Jesus orders Peter to sheathe his sword. After Jesus allows them to bind Him, they roughly drag Him along the way into the dark Kidron Valley.

The disciples scatter. All have deserted Him except John and Peter. They trail far enough behind to follow the Master and yet not close enough to get involved with the troops. After entering the city through the Gate of the Essenes and passing the Pool of Siloam, they rush Him up the steps from the Lower to the Upper City. The climb is sheer agony. After entering the gate of the high priest's family compound, Jesus is taken through the courtyard to the palace of Annas (the father-in-law of Caiaphas and the former high priest). Although deposed by Rome, he still is a powerful manipulator behind the scenes.

JOHN 18:15-24

John is well known in the high priest's palace, often bringing fish for the priestly family or making arrangements for the distribution of fish in Jerusalem. He quickly gains entrance. Peter lags behind, waiting outside until John returns for him. John assures the woman keeping the door that it is all right for this fellow Galilean to enter. The woman recalls seeing Peter with Jesus. When she accuses him of being a disciple, he snaps off a denial.

In the torch-lit reception room of the high priest, Jesus denies nothing of what He has said or done. He declares to Annas that His ministry was carried out in the light, not in dark secretiveness. His sharp reply and acute questioning of the former high priest suddenly seem to put His accusers on trial as He forces them to answer Him defensively. One of the police officers slaps Him across the face and reprimands Him for not showing proper respect for God's representative emeritus. Annas then sends Jesus to Caiaphas for further interrogation.

Back in the courtyard, Peter remains in the shadows warming himself by a charcoal fire. Having been such a vocal and forceful disciple, he is easily recognized by those standing by him. A second time this night Peter denies any connection with Jesus. A servant, however, again questions his identity for this is surely the culprit who cut off the earlobe of his kinsman, Malchus. Peter denies that he is the man. A cock crows announcing in deep night the coming day.

chapter eleven

The Enthronement

A well-rested Jerusalem awakens, ready for final preparations for the feast. During the night, the ceremony of the hunting for leaven has taken place in each home. Lamp in hand, the head of the family has searched every corner to find this potential defiler of the feast. This morning a final check is made so that all that might cause uncleanness is removed from the People's presence.

Mishnah, Pesahim 1:1

The police in the high priest's quarters have as their first duty the transfer of Jesus to the praetorium. The distance is not far, for the two wielders of power over the city are next-door neighbors. They move Jesus before people begin to crowd into the city. It is possible that He might yet be the leaven of a riot during the exciting days of Passover. He must be eliminated so that Rome will not be given an excuse to destroy the center of worship to which the People look for atonement. It is just after dawn, the first hour, when they enter the outer court of the praetorium.

JOHN 18:28

The palace compound is yet another work of that ardent admirer of Rome, Herod the Great. It consists basically of two huge buildings facing each other across a broad courtyard. The building to the south is called the Agrippium after Augustus Caesar's loyal friend who helped him become a world power. The building to the north, the Caesarium, is named after Augustus himself. When Herod's son, Archelaus, was forced to yield the rule of Judea to Rome because of his incompetence, Caesar's representative turned this palace into his official Jerusalem residence.

Josephus, War V, 176-182

Josephus, War I, 402

The buildings possess every imaginable comfort Rome can provide, including immense dining halls, baths, and salons. Every guest room has a special decor fashioned from precious woods and stones gathered from the far corners of the empire. Jerusalem has never before known such a royal residence, not even in the glory days of Solomon. No wonder Herod the Great dedicated this magnificent structure to the king of the world whose control of the area and generosity to him made such splendor possible.

The broad space between the two buildings, where the accusers of Jesus now stand, is a marvelous park area, decked out in all sorts of trees and exotic flowers. Refreshing fountains are interspersed throughout, some designed in the form of animals, with water flowing from their mouths into channels and pools. This adds to the paradisaical effect of this Roman oasis in desert-surrounded Jerusalem. The whole complex, like the Temple, has been built on a platform to raise it even higher on the dominating west ridge overlooking the rest of the city. Because of this elevated foundation, the court between the two buildings is called Gabbatha, *High Place*. The stone paving of the court is designed in varied patterns of mosaics, tiles, and carefully fashioned blocks. To isolate himself from the

John 19:13

Left:
The dome, the
place of sacrifice.

The palace
compound is
another work of
that ardent
admirer of Rome,
Herod the Great.
rest of the city, the great king of the Judeans had a wall constructed around this complex. This was regularly accented with artistic towers which enhance the beauty of the compound and assure its security. The palace area is a fortified city within a city. In at least one respect this former palace of Herod can be compared with that of Solomon, both are more imposing than the House of God.

The small group of the leaders of the People refuse to enter the residence of Pilate, the Caesarium, but wait outside in the court with their prisoner. They must be careful not to come in contact with any uncleanness in this pagan dwelling which would prevent their leadership at the sacrifice this afternoon. The judgment seat of the procurator is placed on the platform in front of the entrance to the Caesarium. Pilate enters and is seated to hear this first item of business. When he asks for the accusation against the prisoner, he is surprised by their request for His execution. When arrangements were made for Jesus' arrest, the Romans probably never thought of such a drastic petition. Pilate goes back into the Caesarium and has Jesus brought to him so that he might interrogate Him privately.

JOHN 18:29-32

Inside the Men's Court of the Temple, a large amount of wood is stacked for the fire that will soon blaze on the altar. Priests, dressed in their fine, white linen robes, inspect the hooks attached to the pillars and walls of the court around the altar upon which the lambs will be hung for flaying. They wait with the Levites for the great sacrifice of the day as they sing the morning praises to God. The gleaming Temple facade towers above the high altar and reflects these

Josephus, War V,
228-230

Ps. 145-150

morning Hallel Psalms back to the crowd of pilgrims who join in offering praise before the footstool of the King of Kings. They begin their praise with the first verse of the Hallel proclaiming: "I will extol You, my God and King!" All their worship is in praise of that glorious King.

In the Caesarium, Pilate's first question concerns a Rome that will tolerate no rival to its dominance over the world. "Are you the king of the Judeans?" Jesus, as always, is in complete control and turns the question back to His imperial interrogator. "Do you say this of your own accord, or did others say it to you?" Suddenly, Caesar's representative is in the dock and himself under interrogation! Pilate's feeble counter is more a plea that Jesus help him understand why He was taken prisoner. Jesus does not answer directly, but rather states that His Kingdom is not of this world. A puzzled Pilate can only retort, "So You are a king?" Jesus explains that His purpose in the world is to bear witness to the truth. Pilate brushes that lofty ideal aside with the sardonic remark, "What is truth?" There is much business for the procurator to complete this day and he certainly is not interested in getting into a discussion of philosophy. Jesus is obviously harmless.

JOHN 18:33-38

Coming out to the leaders waiting before the Caesarium, he declares Jesus innocent. He wants to get on with Rome's normal business on this morning before Passover now that the leaders are present. Each year it is customary that Rome release a prisoner just before the festival. This is a shrewd way of discouraging opposition during such potentially explosive gatherings. He asks if they wish him to release this mock king of the Judeans. Their answer is a further setback for his day. They do not want him to release this quiet, submissive One Who, when given the opportunity to lead the People, so disappointed them. If they are to have a king of the Judeans, they want someone who at least represents the aspirations of the nation. He should be a true freedom fighter who has risked his life for the salvation of the People. He must be one of the imprisoned commandos awaiting execution who Rome derogatorily labels "bandits." One of the chief "bandits" of the freedom fighters is now imprisoned in Jerusalem, Barabbas, *Son* (Bar)-*of-the-father* (Abba). Rome must release *Son-of-the-father,* whom the People want, one who acts for the People's freedom — not this other One Who just talks of His Father.

JOHN 18:38-40

In the district of Bethzatha, outside the city by the Sheep Pool, the first-born lambs have been washed and are ready to be brought into the Temple area for slaughter. Their owners move them with care so that their offering *in no way will be blemished.* There is a chorus of loud bleating as they are about to enter the Sheep Gate near the Antonia. Extra care is also taken that nothing soils their clean, white fleece until they are flayed on the hooks hung from the pillars about the altar area. Then their fine skin will be torn from their backs as they are dressed for the Passover meal.

Pilate, foiled in his attempt to have Jesus released, orders the guards to take Him to the barracks in back of the Caesarium under the towers of Phaesalis and Mariamme. Here the Tenth Legion guards both Caesar's representative and the palaces of the wealthy in the Upper City. The soldiers have waited for this opportune moment to strike back at these rebels who have killed comrades and provoked many bitter skirmishes. Pilate heightens their delight. He orders not the

JOHN 19:1-3

Josephus, War V, 161-175

lightest punishment, beating (which is a mere spanking with sticks), or the next grade of reprimand, flogging (which only results in raising welts), but the harshest of the punishments, scourging.

The soldiers prepare a many-stranded whip, tying small pointed pieces of metal on the end of each strand. Stripping Jesus of His clothes and forcing Him to bend over in submission to Caesar, the administrator with muscles bulging begins to flay away. Each stroke tears away a bit more skin from His back until, when the scourger finally finishes, one can see a speck of exposed bone through the red, pulp-like mass. Then with a delight-filled gesture of cruelty, another soldier who has been eagerly waiting with a handful of salt, smears it over His tortured back. Often the agonized sufferer dies at this point. Yet, somehow Jesus holds on to His life, determined to wait for a later, more perfect *hour*.

The soldiers join in the sadistic fun as they prop Him up by their gaming board, a divided circle that has been scratched into the pavement. The game is simple, involving more chance than skill. Depending on how dice (made of pig bones) land on the circle, points are awarded. This is where the naked, gasping, and shivering Jesus comes into the game. He will be their tally board. Every time someone wins enough points, he gets to dress Him with a piece of mock regal clothing. It is the game of the king. One of the soldiers, anticipating the victory

172

point, makes a crown out of thorns. Despite their jagging and cutting, the soldier fashions a fairly good resemblance of the victory crown worn by Caesar. Caesar's crown, of course, is always made out of green laurel branches, a symbol of life, peace, and above all, his triumph over the world. The suffering, half-dead Joshua-Jesus is then coronated with the brown thorn crown. With malicious enjoyment they press it on His head causing blood to flow freely through His hair and over His dirty, bruised face. Slapping Him around and jeering with cries of Ave! *Hail!* (the acclamation they fervently call out to their Caesar) they tauntingly address Him as "King of the Judeans." Finally, a dirty, discarded purple cloth which resembles a robe is found in the barracks. This final piece of mock royalty is wrapped around Him. The game is finished. Pilate calls for Jesus.

The doors of the Caesarium are opened. The procurator comes out and mounts the platform to announce that he is finished with Jesus. He has shown that He is innocent of any crime. As Jesus emerges from the door, dragged and half carried by brawny soldiers, Pilate points to this broken piece of humanity, naked except for the tearing thorns and purple robe now made darker by oozing blood. "Behold the man!" The expected sympathy for this One scourged almost to death does not come. Demanding more punishment, the cruelest that Rome can inflict, they shout "Crucify Him!" Pilate, exasperated by their reaction, tells them to take Him and crucify Him themselves. Their cry that He should die because He has made Himself the Son of God catches Pilate off guard.

JOHN 19:4-11

Once again he has Jesus brought inside to him. Mighty Rome understands respect for gods, goddesses — and demons. Rome knows that one must be careful not to anger gods or upset spirits over which its intrepid armies have no control. Jesus refuses to answer Pilate's pressing question as to His origin, remaining silent. Pilate is indignant. Will He not even answer the procurator standing in the very praetorium named after the mighty king of Rome, the voice and right arm of Caesar in this city? Does He not know that Caesar has power over life and death? Jesus breaks His silence. He states with all His regal dignity that both Pilate and his Caesar have power over Him now only because God has willed it. The ruthless, iron-willed Pilate is now caught in a moment of weakness. He is not able to lead as he should because he has been too severely challenged.

The brown thorn crown and Caesar's crown of green laurel branches.

Leaving Jesus behind in the Caesarium, he returns to the officials. They now are even more anxious to be rid of this bothersome menace. They want to get to their more pressing duties of the day. Once more Pilate seeks the release of Jesus. This time the impatient elders, noting his hesitation, capitalize on it as they play the raw game of power politics. They issue their ultimatum. If this man is released, Pilate must be reported as not being "Caesar's friend." He will have removed himself from that closed club of Caesar's most ardent supporters. What would then happen to the wealth and the fine life that Caesar allows him to milk out of Judea and Samaria? Would he dare release a rival claimant to the throne, setting himself against Caesar? The procurator's sense of judgment is broken, along with mighty Rome's pride in upholding justice.

JOHN 19:13-16

Pilate has Jesus brought out for the last time. Led by the guards, He half staggers and is half lifted to the platform. As He faces the leaders of the People and Roman troops gathered in the courtyard before the judgment seat, with a majestic serenity accented by His broken body, it seems for a moment that the judgment seat of Caesar is for Him. *He* now stands in judgment of the world.

Ps. 24:7-10

Pilate is now ready to proclaim sentence for the ruler of the world. "Behold your King!" he mocks, pointing to the stooped figure beside him. His words evoke the same cry as before. "Crucify Him!" The last word of Rome from the seat of judgment is but a question, "Shall I crucify your King?" The chief priests and elders have lent their voices day after day to the songs praising God as King over all the earth and every power and principality. They who this afternoon will complete the Passover Hallel psalms by singing: *"It is better to take refuge in the Lord than to put trust in princes,"* now join in Rome's dereliction of its law which it prided itself in upholding. Even worse, they desert their Creator King proclaiming, "We have no king but Caesar!"

Ps. 118:9

It is now about the sixth hour, and the lambs are being gently led from outside the city into the Temple area through the Sheep Gate. The sacrifice must take place earlier this year because Passover and Sabbath coincide. Carefully they guide the lambs over the pavement area to the steps that lead up to the Men's Court surrounding the altar. Some even tenderly carry the innocent ones in their arms. Because not all worshipers are able to enter the inner court at the same time, they are divided into three groups. At the sounding of the Temple trumpet, the shofar, each goes in turn to the altar to offer the sacrifice. As the first group enters, their attention focuses on the altar. It is beautifully crafted, built of the hardest and whitest limestone in the land. The workmanship is exquisite. The entire structure was prepared without the use of iron tools, special care being taken to find perfectly fitting pieces. The top of the altar, marked with four stone horns, rises 22 feet above the priests gathered around its base and is reached by a ramp-like stairway. The altar is built over the rock where the perfect sacrifice, Isaac, was once offered. That son walked to this rock carrying the wood for his own sacrifice. His father, knife and fire in hand, was prepared to offer his only son in place of the lambs if God so directed. Around this rock, lambs are now readied for sacrifice.

Mishnah, Pesahim
4:1-5:9

Gen. 22:1-19

Midrash Rabbah
Gen. 55:7

JOHN 19:17-18

As soon as Pilate leaves the judgment seat at the sixth hour, the soldiers strip the robe from Jesus, pull Him down from the platform, driving and dragging His naked body out of the courtyard to the main street of the Upper City. The

174

horizontal beam of His cross is forced onto His shoulder. As it begins to slip from His weakened hands, He is kicked and slapped until He takes firm enough hold to carry the wood to His execution. Soldiers line the street leading past the upper market place. People, mostly women on their way home to make preparations for receiving the sacrificial lamb, covertly stare at this naked and bleeding excuse of a King Who wears only a painful, mocking crown of thorns. He keeps falling in His utter exhaustion and pain only to be prodded up with a spear as they move Him along the way. The Water Gate, leading out of the city from the wall connecting the huge Phaesalis and Hippicus towers, is opened. Troops stand guard on the towers and along the wall as they watch apprehensively over the crowd gathering to gaze at the spectacle. Outside the gate, the troops immediately turn down the way running between the Pool of the Towers and the hillside supporting the city wall. At the corner of the pool, they start across the broad open space toward the huge rock left at the edge of the quarry.

This hillock of limestone was once part of the same hillside they descend. That part of the abandoned quarry is now a garden area. Its largest and deepest part runs along the base of the high city wall to their right. As they come closer to the hillock, it is clear why this crude limestone mass was left unquarried. The limestone is very poorly formed and crumbly. Its bone-yellow appearance, coupled with the pocked stone and its rounded top, give it the appearance of a *skull,* hence they call it Golgotha. On top of the 22 foot high *Skull,* three stakes, about six feet long, have been inserted into crevices in the fissured rock and secured with stones. They look like horns rising out of the skull. The stone which the builders rejected has been prepared to become the cornerstone for the crucifixion.

Mark 12:10

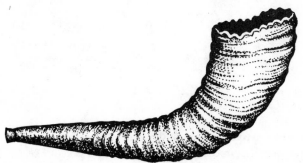

The Temple trumpet, the shofar.

The shofar is blown with a sustained blast, then a wavering one, and then a second sustained blast to signal the beginning of the sacrifice. Each family head in the first group lays his hand on the lamb's head, pulls it back to expose the throat, and slits it with a swift motion. Priests stand by and catch the gushing blood in round-bottomed silver and gold basins. These are then passed from priest to priest up to the altar and thrown against its base. The sacrificed lamb is now hung from the hooks on the pillars. Because of insufficient hooks in this cramped space, some are hung from staffs extended between two men's shoulders. They finish dressing the lambs and remove the parts to be offered upon the altar: kidneys, part of the liver, the fat from around the viscera, and the

They start across
the broad open
space toward the
huge rock left at
the edge of the
Quarry.

crucifixion

fat tail. They are carried to the top of the altar on special trays. Care is taken *not to break any bone* in the process and thus disqualify the sacrifice.

With a blast of the trumpet, a centurion orders Jesus and the two revolutionaries, who will also be crucified in the cramped space above the rock, to be prepared for the crucifixion. Putting their hands on Jesus, soldiers push Him down onto the olive wood crosspiece He has carried, and position Him so that it is under His shoulders. One of the soldiers, taking an iron spike, drives it between the two arm bones by the wrist. He is careful *not to break any bones* so that the agony can be prolonged as long as possible! The other spike is driven into the writhing body with an incessant determination that cannot wait or does not flinch, but rather seems to delight in the frenzied struggle for life. Then Jesus is lifted up to the vertical piece which fits a hole prepared in the crossbeam. They drop the crosspiece on the upright, and His body hangs from His arm bones.

176

Quickly they take up its weight for a moment in order to prevent the bones from breaking, and also to position a seat for Him. The seat is an irritatingly thin piece of acacia wood, splintered so that with every movement of His body, it might tear at Him. His legs are now bent up and a piece of fig wood is pressed across them. A final spike, driven through this wooden clamp binds His feet so that the enthroned One is held in place.

As the first group leaves the Men's Court and the second enters to take their place, they pass the signs that prevent the eyes of the world from observing this most sacred rite. Chisled in limestone for all to see, and set at intervals upon the stone fence surrounding the Sanctuary, the large letters warn in Greek and Latin:

No foreigner is to enter within this balustrade
and embankment around the Sanctuary.
Whoever is caught will have himself to blame
for his death which follows.

Only the men of God's People enter this day behind the walls surrounding the altar. There, as the shofar is again sounded, the second company offers their lambs for the redemption of the people, out of sight of pagans, children, and women.

The soldiers take a sign designed in the official Roman form, which Pilate JOHN 19:19-22 has ordered and nail it to the cross of Jesus. It proclaims, *JESUS OF NAZARETH, KING OF THE JUDEANS*. It is written in Greek, Latin, and

Hebrew for all the world to read — and all the world looks on, so it seems. The place of execution has been well chosen by Rome. People stare from the city walls which form the eastern and southern borders of the open area lying before Golgotha. The way leading north and east from the Upper City passes here. All are shown what it means to go against Rome.

The men gathered around the altar continue the slaying of the lambs as the third group, the last, moves to the foot of the altar. The Hallel Psalms of Passover are again repeated as the last group of men gazes up at the sacrificial smoke rising to the heavens. The sacrificing will soon be completed.

Four women gather at the foot of Golgotha. The men who followed Jesus have all fled or watch fearfully from secluded corners. John is the only man with courage and love enough to bear witness to the end. The faces of the women are JOHN 19:23-27 familiar to those who know Jesus: His aunt; Mary, the wife of Clopas; Mary

The enthronement

John 2:2-4

from Magdala (the fishing village on Galilee's west shore); and Mary, His mother. These five watch as the soldiers divide His garments which have been brought along. This is the soldiers' "tip" for carrying out the execution. They admire His perfectly woven, seamless tunic and decide that it is a shame to rip apart such a fine piece of work. They determine who will be the lucky person to take it by drawing lots.

Jesus looks down to the five who have braved the condemnation of Jerusalem, and even possible death, by associating with Him. Even at this moment of total disgrace, John is not able to turn away from the side of the One he loves. Jesus gasps out to His mother who is being comforted by the beloved disciple, "Behold your son, woman." To John He directs, "Behold your mother." Suddenly the "woman" of Cana at the coming of the *hour* is a "mother." John will care for his new mother for the rest of her life.

178

The final struggle now begins. Jesus is fast tiring, and can no longer pull Himself up to breathe. That very fight for breath keeps tearing Him apart on this torture device which weakens His body until He simply cannot raise Himself to take in air. The spikes by now have gradually sawed their way into Jesus' bones and so ripped His muscles that He can no longer lift His body. The stark sun of this April afternoon hurries the process. It beats at His face, burns His naked body, and draws out the last life-sustaining moisture. Through swollen, cottony lips He rasps, "I thirst." He Who is the Water of Life has now given all for the world. One of the soldiers quickly fills a sponge with vinegar. This drink is mixed with a narcotic mercifully provided by the women of Jerusalem to lessen the pain of the tortured. He uses a leafy stalk of hyssop to lift the sponge to His lips. Following this, the struggle is over. Jesus suffocates, proclaiming with His last breath, "It is completed." *John 4:13-14, 7:37*

The men in the last company drive their sharp knives into the lambs, opening the arteries. Warm blood gushes out. At the first Passover, hyssop had been dipped in this and used to sprinkle the blood on the doorposts. Now priests, their white robes splattered crimson, place the last of the bowls beneath the wound to catch the life of the lamb. This is conveyed from priest to priest. Finally, the last in the row throws it against a now thoroughly bloodied altar base. This last group seems to be wading in blood as cistern water is mixed with it to clean the area before the blood congeals. The air hangs thick with the sickening sweet smell of warm, newly lost life. *Ex. 12:22*

The day is now drawing to a close. The soldiers are informed that the bodies must not be allowed to remain on the crosses on the Sabbath. It may take another day or so for these strong revolutionaries to lose their battle for breath. To hurry the process and to assure no recuperation, a soldier methodically wields a hammer, smashing the leg bones of the two on either side of Jesus, and sending a shiver of sympathetic pain through even the most callous onlooker. When the soldier turns to the central cross, he realizes that this One is no longer a problem. Jesus is dead. There is no need to break His legs, only to run a spear into His side to ensure death's total victory. As the soldier drives the sharp spearhead into His side, wine-red blood and water gush out, flowing down over the sign, "King of the Judeans" and onto the skull-like rock below. Tiny rivulets of blood form and flow toward the rock's side, covering the earth. The soldiers could care less about cleaning it up or washing it away. It simply sinks into the world. *JOHN 19:31-37*

The last of the flayed lambs are taken gently from the crosspieces between the men's shoulders and from the hooks fastened to walls and pillars. Care is taken that not one of the bones is broken, as Moses prescribed. The legs are folded carefully into the body cavity which is then wrapped in its own skin. Carrying the sacrifices, these men are joined by those waiting in the Temple area as they now leave together, dispersing to their homes before the Sabbath begins. There the body of the lamb is carefully washed and prepared for roasting by being rubbed with salt. A spit made of a pomegranate branch is put through it and the limbs are bound into the body. As it roasts, family and close friends begin to gather in the solemnly lighted home. Here they recall the Exodus of the People from captivity, when blood on every doorpost and the eating of the lamb redeemed the People from the terrible night of death. They remember not only *Ex. 12:46*

Mishnah, Pesahim 7:1-8:7

A lamp burns in the niche above the bench.

the past, but their present bondage to Rome which controls their beloved city and the Holy Place this night. They wait for an anointed one who will come to remove from their midst all threat of slavery and death as the bread of blessing is broken and passed and they begin to partake of the lamb.

The two fighters for liberation, still struggling for life, are torn away from their crosses and dragged to a prison to await impending death. Jesus hangs alone, drooped over almost as in submission to the world. Yet, even in death, that world seems strangely under His control. One of the men who stayed in the shadows watching this sacrifice of one Man for the People was Joseph, a rich man from the hometown of Samuel, Arimathea. He is the owner of the garden beside which the crucifixions have taken place. Recently he purchased this valuable former stone quarry for his family tomb. The first burial chamber has just been cut into the limestone wall of the quarry which faces Golotha, of which it was once a part. Being of the upper class and having many an opportunity for business with the procurator, he easily gains permission for a secret meeting with Pilate at which he requests permission to bury Jesus in his family tomb. Permission is quickly granted.

JOHN 19:38-42

The crowds are now gone. Those on their way home or heading for encampments avoid coming any closer to the dead One for fear of being made unclean. Helped by Nicodemus (who has been watching from the shadows not only this afternoon, but for several years) and the few soldiers left on cleanup detail, Joseph unfastens Jesus from the wood and slowly lowers His body. Lifting Him down from the rock, they carry Jesus the 25 yards to the tomb entrance. Tenderly they lay out His body, carefully washing away the blood and cleansing it of the dirt of abuse. Olive oil is mixed with perfume and rubed on Him to prevent the stench of death. Linen bands are brought and He is carefully wrapped. With one last look at the features that have brought so much life to them, they cover His face with a napkin of linen which is then bound over the head.

Jesus is then passed through the small, square opening of the tomb into the dark chamber. The bench on the right side of the tomb is cut beautifully from the rock with an arched ceiling chiseled in the stone. A lamp burns in the niche above the bench illuminating the bound One below. Joseph spares no expense, ordering that 75 pounds of spice be brought and packed into the tomb chamber to prevent any smell from escaping from the tomb. Joseph gives a royal burial to his King who now sleeps in death. A stone is set in place to block the opening of the tomb. Sabbath, the day God rested at the completion of the first week of the Good Creation, begins.

chapter twelve

He Reigns

In that last moment of darkness when night can no longer hold back the first light of day, Mary, the faithful one from Magdala by the Sea of Galilee, who bore witness to the end, approaches to weep where her Beloved lies. She looks toward the stone at the tomb entrance and finds it removed. As the sun rises over the Mount of Olives its rays turn the chamber's darkness into light. Without moving any closer, she turns and runs to John and Peter to report the removal of the Rabbi's body.

JOHN 20:1 *—31*

John 1:1-5

John 19:25

JOHN 20:2-10

As they approach the garden area and see the opening, the two disciples break into a sprint with John reaching the tomb first. Standing under the shallow porch cut into the hillside in front of the chamber's small entrance, John bends down to the yard-high door to look at the bench on the right where the Anointed One had lain. John is the first to see that He is not there and that no one has stolen the body, at least in its wrapped form. The bands of death have been left in the tomb. Someone has carefully folded and laid them on the vacated bench. The cloth which covered His head is there also neatly rolled up and placed to the side. Before John can move closer, Peter arrives right behind him and crawls into the chamber. John then enters. As the beloved disciple stands in the tomb which no longer needs lamps to dispel darkness and breathes the fresh air that makes the masking spices unnecessary, he suddenly understands. Death has not been transferred to another place. Death has been conquered! In awe they return home.

Mary, who followed behind, stays to mourn although her tears are now meaningless. She bends to look through an opening that no longer separates her from Life. The darkness inside is turned to light so she can clearly see the discarded bands of death. Her weeping is even called into question by two angels now seated on either side of the bench. In her grief, Mary sees nothing. She can only mumble over and over again that they have taken away her Master.

JOHN 20:11-18

As she begins to straighten, half turning from the small opening, she senses someone standing by her. In her grief she does not fully turn to look the stranger in the face when He asks her the same question as did the heavenly messengers, "Woman, why are you weeping?" At such an early hour this could only be the gardener of Joseph's tomb. As she pleads to be shown where Jesus is, Mary thinks only of a corpse. With all the warmth and familiarity of its ring, Jesus calls this bewildered, wandering sheep of His flock by name. She *knows* His voice and cries, "Rabboni," *"Teacher!"* Jesus tells her not to cling to Him for He is now *leading the way* to the Father. She is to go and tell His followers.

John 10:3-4

John 1:18

Left:
The tomb.

The Galilee is a
land of promise as
the fishing season
draws to an end.

Gen. 2:7

Later that day Jesus appears to His flock. Thomas, however, is away from the fold. The disciples are herded together in a room whose door is closed against the threatening forces who, by now, know of the empty tomb. He brings them peace and the commission to be His living body in the world. As in the first week of the Creation, the Spirit was breathed into lifeless clay to create human life, now the disciples become new Adams as He breathes new Life into them.

JOHN 20:19-31

John 11:16

A skeptical Thomas questions their report of the Risen One's presence, demanding to touch with his hands the mark of the spear left in His side, and to see with his eyes the place where the spikes penetrated His wrists (expressed in Hebrew, *hands*). After eight days, Jesus provides that opportunity. The one who followed to death in spite of the hazards of the way now does not need to reach out and touch, but exclaims, "My Lord and my God!" Jesus assures them that His blessing goes beyond the inner circle in this closed room. Blessed indeed will be those who have not seen with their eyes or touched with their own hands, but seeing and feeling the way through the reports of others come to faith in Him.

JOHN 21:1-3

New Life in Judea cannot be contained there. The disciples have brought that Life to the Galilee as they return back into the everyday world. Following the Passover, the Galilee is a land of promise as the fishing season draws to a close. John, James, Peter, Thomas, and Nathanael have just finished one of those discouraging nights at the season's end. Their nets are empty.

At dawn, as they are about to return, they notice a figure outlined on the stone-cut dock of Heptapegon a hundred yards from them. He asks about their success. Not expecting Him here in the midst of their daily labor, they do not realize at first that it is Jesus. When they explain that their efforts have been futile, He indicates where the fish are, for Jesus has the advantage of height over the water. They drop their nets, which are immediately filled almost to breaking. John, again seeing through set expectations and into a New World, realizes that it is the Risen One. When he cries out that it is the Master, Peter moves with all the vigor his powerful body can muster. He pulls on his clothes and jumps overboard into this shallow area of the lake. With water spraying from both sides, he rushes to the Risen One. JOHN 21:4-8

Jesus has prepared a breakfast of fish and bread. He calls for them to bring more fish to the banquet. Over the water, the Gennesaret Plain, Mount Arbel, JOHN 21:9-14 and *the* Mount form the background for this feast after the Passover. There are 153 fish in the net, a perfect catch fishermen would say — a third always goes to the boat, a third to the fishermen, and a third to the provider of nets. As they breakfast on these miniature leviathans and freshly baked, manna-sweet bread, they feast their eyes on the presence of the Risen One. JOHN 21:15-19

Jesus turns to Peter asking:

"Simon, son of John, do you love Me more than these?"

Peter, always ready with that undeniable answer, replies:

"Yes, Master, you know that I love You."

Turning thoughts back to winter when the frail, new life of the flock can so easily be lost for lack of loving care, Jesus tells Peter:

"Feed My lambs."

Again, a second time, Jesus raises the question:

The stone-cut dock of Heptapegon.

185

"Simon, son of John, do you love Me more than these?"

Peter's affirmation doubly removes any denial:

"Yes, Master, you know that I love you."

Jesus directs him:

"Pasture My sheep."

That is the work that the fishermen now enter as the season of toil on the sea is completed and the creatures of the depths have been caught to provide food for the People. The season of shepherding now begins. Spring is the time to take the young lambs of winter (who need more than pabulum) out into the world. They must be directed to its goodness that they might grow and become strong through the spring and summer.

Yet again, Jesus presses the question as if to assure no denial of Peter's love, asking:

"Simon, son of John, do you love Me?"

John 13:38 Although hurt that Jesus would press the question a third time, Peter knows that he was forced that many times to deny the One he so loved. He affirms in the brightness of the new morning's light:

"Master, you know everything, you know that I love you!"

Jesus replies that he must care for the sheep that will be so near death from starvation in those dark days of late fall before the resurrecting rain brings new life to the land. In those months when food must be carried to the sheep and they must be doubly cared for as they bear the lambs of the spring, He urges:

"Feed My sheep."

To go to the flock and give one's life in bringing them nourishment through all seasons from youth to old age — to take the things that have been seen, heard, and touched, and feed the flock with them that their hunger might be ended, their thirst quenched, and their joy complete — this is *following the Way.*

Appendixes

Bethany of Peraea

In the third century A.D., Origen, a scholar of the early Church, begins the long detour around the need for locating Bethany in Peraea by substituting the name "Bethabara." He admits that the most ancient manuscripts read "Bethany," but makes the change because he could not find a village by this name when visiting the area *(Commentary on John,* VI, 204-207). Bethabara is the place where pilgrims remembered John baptizing Jesus in the Jordan in the first three Gospels, the Synoptics. Surprisingly, many ancient and modern commentators have blindly followed this detour. Some, like Chrysostom *(Homily,* XVII), even claim that the *more accurate* texts of John read "Bethabara!" A lingering uncertainty is demonstrated by Jerome who, in his commentary on John, follows Origen with "Bethabara," but retains "Bethany" in his Latin translation!

This problem stems from an error that has been made throughout the history of the Church — that of mixing the accounts of the Synoptics with the Johannine tradition. This amalgamating tendency ignores the fact that the world of each Gospel is different. John emphasizes that the opening scene is located in the district *on the other side of the Jordan,* i.e., Peraea. He states that John baptizes there, but *never* mentions the baptism of Jesus by John. In the opening chapter there is *no* activity at the Jordan River. It is incorrect to seek or discuss the "baptismal place" of Jesus when discussing John's Gospel, as do Dalman *(Sacred Sites and Ways,* 87). N. Glück *(River Jordan,* 245), and others. The Madaba map locates Bethabara on the *west side* of the Jordan further underscoring the improbability of the place that evidently was shown to pilgrims, for this is not even in Peraea!

Where is Bethany of Peraea? Origen's dilemma is ours. Nobody has definitively located it. Oddly, in the former area of Peraea, most ruins of ancient settlements do not retain any hint of previous names, although surveys indicate many villages in this region in the Roman period.

Bethany should be located in the area of Peraea across from Jericho. This is closer to the wilderness from which the Baptist cries, and is also an area where there is good tradition for fixing the activity of the Baptist. This locale also suits better the movement found in the account of the resurrection of Lazarus (John 11). This area was well populated, providing an audience not only of permanent residents, but also of those coming to escape the cold, wet winter of the highlands.

We locate Bethany near the Wadi Abu Aruba, which carries much water in winter. About a half mile from this wadi is the sector of el Kharrar with a good spring. It is about a mile from the traditional area of John's ministry at the Jordan River. This area is elevated, giving the impression of a small podium on the plain, which apparently led to its designation as the place from which Elijah ascended to heaven.

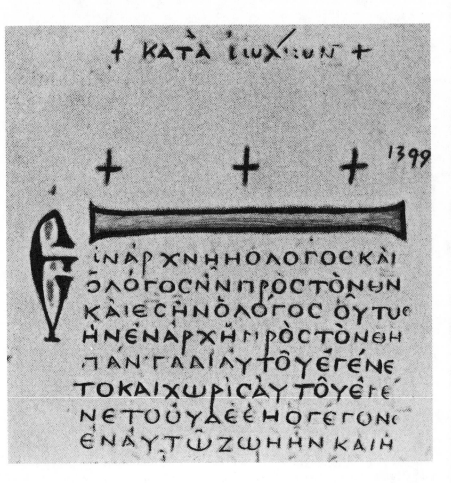

Beginning of the Gospel of St. John in the Vatican Codex (fourth century).

The Chronology of John's Gospel

When studying the setting of John's Gospel, one must be aware of the season of the year in which events take place. The winter world of the Jordan Valley contrasts dramatically from summer. The various scenes Jesus points out, or the work of the farmers He describes in His teaching, differ radically from February to October. That John wants us to note the time of year is clear from the great care he takes in specifically designating feasts. The feasts do follow in correct order as John describes Jesus' ministry and they fit His comments. Because of this interest in time, we should not be surprised that John gives a date from which the events of the Gospel can be arranged. In 2:20, the Temple is described as in the forty-sixth year of its construction. Josephus gives two dates for the beginning of Herod's Temple, but that of the eighteenth year of Herod's reign (20/19 B.C.) is accepted as accurate (Josephus, *Antiquities,* XV, 380). Reckoning from this, the date of the cleansing of the Temple in John's Gospel would be Passover, A.D. 28. Since Passover is calculated by the moon, it is possible for the astronomer to determine the date of Passover for any year. Passover in A.D. 28 was on April 29, a late Passover. If the Gospel is treated as a whole, no matter what theory of editing is used, it is possible to reconstruct from this peg a rough chronological sequence of events as the Gospel now stands in the canon.

For Further Study:

K. Schoch, "Christi Kreuzigung am 14 Nisan," *Biblica, 9* (1928) 48-56, J. K. Fotheringham, "The Evidence of Astronomy and Technical Chronology for the Date of the Crucifixion," *Journal of Theological Studies,* 35 (1934) 146-162.

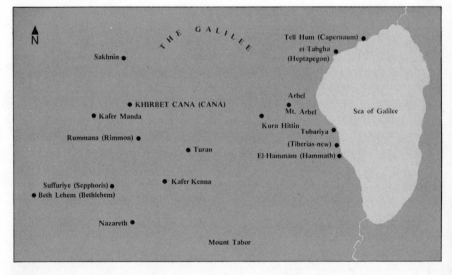

THE GALILEE

N

Sakhnin ●

Tell Hum (Capernaum) ●
et-Tabgha
(Heptapegon)

Arbel
●
Mt. Arbel

● KHIRBET CANA (CANA)

● Kafer Manda

Sea of Galilee

Kurn Hittin
Tubariya
(Tiberias-new)
El-Hammam (Hammath)

Rummana (Rimmon) ●

● Turan

Suffuriye (Sepphoris) ●
● Beth Lehem (Bethlehem)

● Kafer Kenna

Nazareth ●

Mount Tabor

Cana

Cana is probably the least visited New Testament site in the Holy Land. Rarely does a group hike the three miles from the nearest village, Kafer Manda, to the hill upon which the village once rested. Although inhabitants and pilgrim bands have deserted the site, the name still remains. The hilltop is known to its Arabic-speaking neighbors as Kirbet Cana, *Ruin of Cana.* Actually, Cana had a long history before its demise about 1838. Some claim that the Cana in Joshua ˙19:28 once rested on this hill, although most are inclined to locate that *Reed* in southern Lebanon. Kirbet Cana was a thriving center in the days of the divided kingdom. Tiglath-Pileser wrought terrible destruction in this area in 739 B.C. (This is referred to in Isaiah 9:1-2.) The fragmentary report of his conquest of the Galilee notes that 650 prisoners were taken from Cana.

Cana's importance during the revolt against Rome is indicated by Josephus who used this village as one of his headquarters *(Life,* 86-91). In the Byzantine period we find more reports of pilgrims visiting Cana than Nazareth! As would be expected, a church was built there. Interestingly, St. Willibrand reports it still standing in 754. This is about a century after the Muslims gained control of Palestine. With the arrival of the Crusaders, the beginning of the end of Cana as a site for pilgrimage was marked. Pilgrims record visits to the site which corresponds to the present Kirbet Cana, but there are also accounts of visits to another site. This was the result of rerouting the main road to the Sea of Galilee. Instead of passing by Sepphoris, it connected Tiberias with Nazareth which was an important Crusader center. There is a village along this route called Kafer Kenna, *Village of the Daughter-in-Law.* To foreign ears this sounded enough like Cana that unquestioning pilgrims accepted this as the authentic site, rather than Kirbet Cana which is five miles from this route. The greatest encouragement for the shift to Kafer Kenna came as recently as 1616 when the Franciscan, Quaresmius, decided to follow the Greek Orthodox in officially designating this as the true site. By 1874, the Franciscans managed to purchase the mosque located where it was felt the sign had taken place. The excavations that followed, however, uncovered not the expected Byzantine church, but rather a synagogue from that period! The Franciscans have built a church over this ruin.

The list of Old and New Testament geographers and their arguments supporting Kirbet Cana as the site of the first sign is too long to review. C. Kopp, a Roman Catholic scholar who has devoted many years to the study of New Testament geography, has made the most extensive study of the two sites and provides a good bibliography in support of Kirbet Cana. Kirbet Cana still awaits the archaeologists, although surface investigation shows clearly that it was occupied from the days of the Judges until the last century.

Left:
Central lower
Galilee.

The site was too dangerous to visit early in this century, being inhabited by robber bands. Today it peacefully awaits those willing to walk a bit to enjoy the truly magnificent view of the Asochis Plain and central Galilee.

For further study:

C. Kopp, *The Holy Places of the Gospels* (New York: Herder, 1963) 143-154. For complete notation, see the unabridged German version, *Die heiligen Stätten der Evangelien* (Regensburg: Pustet, 1959). For the Franciscan position, see P. B. Bagatti, "Le Anticheta de Kh. Qana di Kefer Kenna in Galilee," *Liber Annus* (1964-65) 251-292.

Judeans not Jews

The term *Ioudaioi* occurs 69 times in John's Gospel, compared to five or six in the others. Should it be translated "Judeans" or "Jews"? The choice makes a difference in understanding the Gospel's intent. The usual translation, "Jews," has even turned John into a tool for bigots to use against modern Rabbinic Judaism. "Jews" indicates to modern readers a religious group, whereas "Judeans," refers to a people from an historical-geographical area. Any equation of *Ioudaioi* with a present-day religious group is wrong. Before the destruction of Jerusalem in A.D. 70, the People of God living in the area of Judea (or who understood proper worship as being centered in Judea) were called *Ioudaioi*. They belonged to several groups, including Sadducees, Pharisees, Essenes, various Baptist groups, mystics, secularized Herodians, and a group which is far too often forgotten — Christians. There were also many converts who may have never seen Judea, but regarded it as the homeland of their faith. One of the most important results of recent study of the first century is to shatter the simplistic picture of "Jews" in Palestine and "pagans" in the outside world.

Prior to A.D. 70, there was not a pure, neatly structured "Judaism." Pagans or Samaritans who had no interest in the internal disputes of the people loyal to Jerusalem lumped all the groups together under the same name, *Ioudaioi*. Like "Samaritan," the term carried not only a religious but also a geographic meaning. John's Gospel shows too great a familiarity with Palestine to allow the translator to dismiss his use of *Ioudaioi* as a vague term.

The word *Ioudaioi* must be understood in terms of the general geographical structure of John's Gospel. The Gospel is partly organized in terms of regions: Judea, Samaria, and the Galilee, which are contrasted to each other according to their acceptance or rejection of Jesus. The Gospel constantly shifts between the Galilee and Judea.

There are even more precise indications that the term *Ioudaioi* should be interpreted geographically. In 3:22, Jesus is described as going into "the land of Judea." In verse 25, there is a discussion with a person from that area, a "Judean." The same proximity is seen in 7:1. "After this Jesus went about in the Galilee; He would not go about in Judea, because the *Judeans sought to kill Him*." A reference to the "Judean" feast of Tabernacles (one must not forget there were also "Samaritan" feasts!) in 7:2 is followed in 7:3 by a clear indication of geography, as His brothers urge Him to "leave here and go to Judea." Similarly in 11:7-8, "Let us go into Judea again," is followed by the response: "the *Judeans* were but now seeking to stone you. ... "

In fact, when the term is not understood geographically, unnecessary problems are created. The question as to what is meant by Jesus' *homeland* in John 4:44 is no problem at all when *Ioudaioi* is understood geographically.

Jesus' loyalty is to Judea, which is His *homeland*. Thus Jesus can say to the Samaritan woman in 4:22, who has addressed Him in geographic terms ("me, a woman of Samaria"), that salvation is from the "Judeans." It is One coming from Judean Jerusalem Who speaks with her as geographical comparisons are made between the centers of worship in Judea and Samaria (4:20-21).

John's failure to differentiate between the "Judeans" living in the Galilee and the other Galileans is not difficult to understand. The term "Galilean" was commonly used by the Judeans living in the south in a derogatory way for those who chose to live in the north, as in 7:52. Because of their proximity to the Jerusalem Sanctuary, they felt themselves somehow better. We note this feeling also in the designation of Judeans living in the west as "Greeks." Persons living outside their homeland know well how their compatriots refer to them derogatorily by classing them with the people with whom they have chosen to live. It is also not surprising that "Galileans" of "Judean" background refer to people in the south as "Judeans," although they themselves are of the same background. Those who have lived in a foreign country for only a short time often find themselves referring to their compatriots as their neighbors do.

For further study:

M. Lowe, "Who Were the IOYΔAIOI?" *Novum Testamentum,* 18 (1977) 101-130.

For the importance of regions in John see W. A. Meeks, "Galilee and Judea in the Fourth Gospel," *Journal of Biblical Literature,* 85 (1966) 159-169.

A critique of this position, as well as further bibliography can be found in W. D. Davies, *The Gospel and the Land* (Berkeley: Un. of California Press, 1974) 321-331.

The Setting of Herod's Temple

Any picture of the Temple area* is drawn from a combination of archaeological finds around the Haram esh-Sharif (the Muslim name for the former Temple area), a few, very rough representations of the Sanctuary on coins, reports found in Josephus and the *Mishnah,* and a tremendous amount of imagination! All traces of the Sanctuary have disappeared. The Arch of Titus in Rome does give us an idea of the furnishings of the Sanctuary.

The space included in the Temple area is known due to the sturdy Herodian walls that still enclose the Haram esh-Sharif. There is also a reference point in this area for beginning a reconstruction — the stone now covered by the Dome of the Rock. Even these important, positively indentified items are not problem-free. The Haram esh-Sharif does not fit either written description of the Temple area's size. This is a result of the lengthening of the northern side of the Temple area by the Muslims who removed part of the natural rock platform upon which the Antonia fortress was built.

Many scholars consider the rock under the Dome of the Rock with its grotto to be the base of the altar. Others claim it is the location of the Holy of Holies, the innermost room in the Sanctuary. For our reconstruction, we accept this as the base of the altar. *(not both)*

The chances of obtaining a clearer archaeological picture of the Haram esh-Sharif, the third most holy place of Islam, are almost nil. However, those responsible for the Haram have allowed careful study of its underground passageways and substructures.

There has been a long history of archaeological activity outside the Haram. One of the first to describe and study the area was the American Biblical geographer, H.E. Robinson, who visited Jerusalem during the first half of the last century. Robinson's arch is named for him. This was the beginning of the first arch which supported the grand staircase descending from the Royal Porch.

---

*A distinction is made in the New Testament between the *naos,* the Temple building and altar area before it, and the *hieron,* the entire enclosed area around the Temple building. It is unfortunate that English translations of the New Testament seldom make this distinction, simply translating both words as "Temple." In our text, such terms as "Sanctuary" and "House of God" are used when the Greek reads *naos.* "Temple area" or "Temple mount" is used for *hieron.* One should be aware that John 1:14 uses a verbal form of *skene* which means "tabernacle" or "tent." Thus, we have translated the verse, "He tabernacled among us." When Jesus replaces the House of God in chapter 2, this brings us back to 1:14, as well as to the Exodus and the Jerusalem of David's day when there was no building. God's Glory was present in a movable tent that had no fixed point, such as that which the Judeans have labored 46 years to make fast. Jesus is the Tabernacle, *skene,* moving wherever God's People might be (John 4:21-24).

In 1864, the Frenchman M. DeVogue published *Le Temple de Jerusalem*. This invaluable work contains the classic reconstruction of Herod's Temple. Almost every model of the Temple is based on his reconstruction, as are our pictures.

C. Wilson carried the investigations underground in 1867-68. He discovered the first arch of the bridge that crossed the Tyropoeon Valley to the Upper City. It is still called Wilson's Arch in his honor.

Between 1867 and 1879, C. W. Warren literally *dug* into the study of the area with a series of tunnels and shafts. His shaft by the eastern wall of the Haram traced the structure to its base, giving us a true impression of its original height. While tunneling under the area near Robinson's Arch, he found the piers that supported the top of the staircase of which the arch was the beginning. He also helped clarify the subterranean picture of the Haram itself by careful study of all its substructures.

K. M. Kenyon was the first to carry out a modern, carefully controlled archaeological excavation in the area outside the Haram. During her archaeological study of Jerusalem from 1961 until 1967, she opened an area near the southeast corner of the Haram. Her work shows why excavations in this area demand very careful digging so that the layers of each period of destruction, which are intermingled with others, might be properly understood. In the small

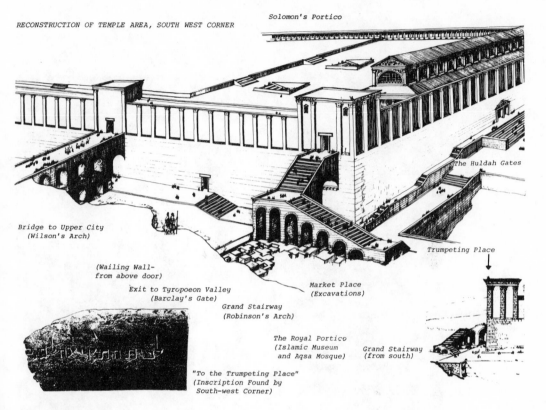

RECONSTRUCTION OF TEMPLE AREA, SOUTH WEST CORNER

Solomon's Portico

The Huldah Gates

Bridge to Upper City
(Wilson's Arch)

Trumpeting Place

(Wailing Wall-
from above door)

Exit to Tyropoeon Valley
(Barclay's Gate)

Market Place
(Excavations)

Grand Stairway
(Robinson's Arch)

The Royal Portico
(Islamic Museum
and Aqsa Mosque)

Grand Stairway
(from south)

"To the Trumpeting Place"
(Inscription Found by
South-west Corner)

area she studied, she could only conclude that Herod had quarried this area before building structures above it.

From 1968 until 1977, M. Mazar cleared the area along the entire southern side of the Haram and that under Robinson's Arch. Besides exposing all of the piers of the grand staircase connected to Robinson's Arch, he uncovered the monumental stairway leading to the Huldah Gates and part of the market Place in front of the Temple platform. Parts of the Royal Porch and its fine decorations were found in the ruins. They fell here when the Temple area was destroyed in A.D. 70. An inscription was even found that had marked the place on the tower above the grand stairway where the trumpeter announced the beginning of Sabbaths and festivals.

Some special studies have also helped complete our picture of the Royal Porch. R. Grafman, after studying the measurements of Robinson's Arch, has determined that the foot used by Herod measured exactly 1.02 English feet. This measurement was used not only for the Temple, but other Herodian buildings as well. Grafman has found that Josephus is more accurate than many had thought ("Herod's Foot and Robinson's Arch," *Israel Exploration Journal,* 20 [1970].

C. Corbett did a carefull study of the ancient entryways under the Haram area. His work helps us reconstruct the Huldah Gate passageways as they were

The right Huldah Gate now called the Triple Gate

in the days of Jesus ("Some Observations on the Gateway to the Herodian Temple in Jerusalem," *Palestine Exploration Quarterly,* 84 [1952] 7-14).

The area north of the Haram was first studied by Ch. Clermont-Ganneau (1873-74). L. H. Vincent followed his studies, describing the Antonia as part of the present-day Sisters of Zion Convent. After careful study of this basement, P. Benoit has challenged Vincent's conclusions. The ruins in the basement of the Sisters of Zion Convent are not older than the so called "Ecce Homo" arch that spans the street in front of the convent. This arch has been positively dated to the period of Hadrian, i.e., second century A.D. The Antonia is now understood to be smaller than the reconstruction by Vincent. Just as described by Josephus, it was a tower built on the table of rock where the Omariyya School is today, and extended out into the present Haram area.

The only pictorial remains of the Sanctuary are rough representations of its facade on coins. They show four columns reaching the entire length of the facade, with a high, wide door between them. A painting from Dura Europa, a glass from the catacombs in Rome, and a lamp with an impression of the building on it, all show the Temple with a gabled roof. However, it is questionable if these are drawn from earlier pictures of the Sanctuary. They may simply be copied from pagan temples the artists knew.

Finally, we have written accounts. However, that of the tractate *Middoth* in the *Mishnah* does not agree with Josephus' account. *Middoth* seems to follow an idealized plan of the Temple as found in Ezekiel, instead of describing Herod's Temple. The tractate was written c. A.D. 150, when there were few, if any, eyewitnesses left. Josephus' description is the best we have. He served as a general for the People of God at the beginning of the revolt against Rome, defecting early in the war. He knew the Temple well, being of a priestly family.

The description of the Temple area and Sanctuary in *War*, V, 184-247, is the best account we have. *Antiquities*, XV, 391-425, is Josephus' other general description of the area. His account of Solomon's Temple in *Antiquities*, VIII, 63-98 is also helpful. Many of the details which he adds to the Biblical account are probably taken from the Sanctuary he knew. The best description of the Royal Porch is found in *Antiquities*, XV, 410-417. Paragraph 410 describes the grand staircase descending from the Royal Porch.

For further study:

K. M. Kenyon, *Digging Up Jerusalem* (New York: Praeger, 1974).

J. Simon, *Jerusalem in the Old Testament* (Leiden: Brill, 1952) 344-436. This is a good review of the studies on the Temple area and has a good bibliography.

Jerusalem Revealed, an Israel Exploration Society publication, 1975, is the best review in English of the archaeological work in Jerusalem in the past decade.

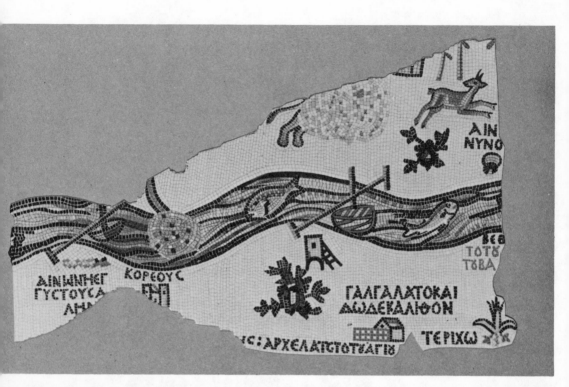

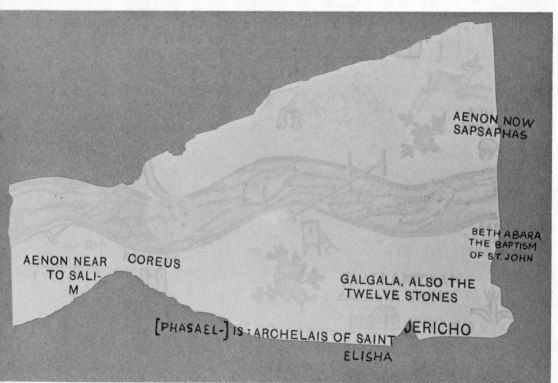

AENON NOW
SAPSAPHAS

AENON NEAR COREUS
TO SALI-
M

BETH ABARA
THE BAPTISM
OF ST. JOHN

GALGALA. ALSO THE
TWELVE STONES

[PHASAEL-] IS : ARCHELAIS OF SAINT
ELISHA

JERICHO

Aenon

Aenon is not frequently mentioned by early pilgrims. Those who do, usually locate it in the Bethshan area, as does the Madaba map. W. F. Albright *(Harvard Theological Review,* 17 [1924] 193-194) locates this Byzantine site at Kirbet Um´ el-Umdan. Pilgrims were uncomfortable with this location. The Madaba map, for instance, also locates Aenon across from Jericho, near the place where Jesus was baptized in the Synoptic accounts. It seems that most early commentators can only picture the Baptist's ministry near the Jordan. Yet, there seems little point in the comment that there "was much water in that place" (John 3:23) if it was located by the river.

Left:
Parts of the
Madaba map.

Most English versions of John's Gospel, unfortunately, omit the definite article before Salem which is found in all the Greek manuscripts. There is no known major city near Bethshan in the Roman period which could be designated as *the* Salem. There is a Salem dating before the Roman period in the plain before ancient Shechem. This Samaritan village was important because (according to the ancient Greek version of Genesis 33:18) Jacob first stayed here. Samaritan tradition also associated this Salem with Melchizedek. It was such an important village in the first century that its name was applied to the plain in front of Ebal and Gerizim. Albright suggests locating Aenon to the north of this Salem, in the area of ancient Tirzah (Tell el-Far'a). R. deVaux points out in the excavation report on Tell el-Far'a that there is a Kirbet Aenon north of this site. In spite of its name *Ruin of Springs,* Kirbet Aenon has not one spring! DeVaux feels that the people from the area of Tell el-Far'a moved to Kirbet Aenon because of malaria, taking the name of the area with them. We suggest that the area of Aenon may be more exactly located in the Wadi Beidan just south of Tell el-Far'a and below the plain of the Salem. This area has more than twelve springs. It is difficult to determine exactly what John means by "near" the Salem. Bethany is mentioned as "near Jerusalem" (John 11:18), being about two miles away. Wadi Beidan is four miles from Salem by road. The direct distance is three miles. It is less than two miles from the edge of the Salem Plain.

See C. H. Scobie, *John the Baptist* (Philadelphia: Fortress Press, 1964), Chapter X "The Samaritan Ministry" for bibliography.

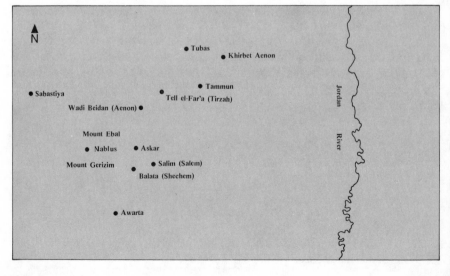

Sychar and the Samaritan Holy Place

The two possibilities for the location of Sychar — Balata and Askar — have been much debated. Balata (near the ruins of Shechem) was the site of a village in the Roman period, according to the excavator of Shechem, G. E. Wright *(Zeitschrift des deutschen Palästina-Vereins,* 83 [1967] 199-202). It possesses a fine spring located about 300 yards from Jacob's well. Askar, also a village in the Roman period, is located about three-quarters of a mile north of Jacob's well. It also has a spring. Those favoring Askar are a slight majority. W. F. Albright has challenged the choice of Askar based on similarity of names, a frequent argument for Askar.

There are several reasons for the choice of Balata in the reconstruction. After a hike that has left the disciples tired and hungry, it seems rather odd that they would walk four times the distance necessary to get food, as those who have hiked to Jacob's well can attest! The Greek phrase "to the city" indicates that Jacob's well is in the region of Sychar. It would be odd to describe Jacob's well as near a village which is some distance from it, and ignore its neighboring village. Sychar is said to be "near the field which Jacob gave Joseph." This field lies before the ruins of Shechem which is much closer to modern Balata than Askar. Since Sychar is a derogatory name, it would make sense for the proper name to have a special meaning for Samaritans. *Oak* probably was the Samaritan name, even as it is today. It proudly recalls Abraham's and Jacob's visits to Shechem. In fact, Jerome locates Sychar at Shechem, and a Syrian manuscript of John actually reads "Shechem" for Sychar. That the grave of Joseph is not mentioned (although located near Balata) is not surprising. The Judean work, *Testament of Joseph* 20:6, and the Judean Josephus, *Antiquities* II: 199-200, bury him at Judean Hebron. There are still two tombs for Joseph — one near Jacob's well, and the other at Hebron. This use of Judean language helps to emphasize Jesus' shattering of expectations by His Samaritan ministry.

It is not clear if there was a temple on Mount Gerizim in A.D. 28. The last account of the temple is that of its destruction by John Hyrcanus in B.C. 129 (Josephus, *Antiquities* XIII, 256). The sacred area was most probably on the summit which can be seen throughout Samaria. R. Bull who excavated the temple Hadrian built 430 feet below the summit for his *New City* (Neapolis, or today, Nablus), feels this may be the site of the Samaritan temple *(Biblical Archaeologist* 38 [1975] 54-59). His arguments do not take into full account that Hadrian had to use this lower peak because the summit of Gerizim is difficult to see from Nablus.

The church of the Byzantines on the summit may well be located on the site of the first-century holy place or temple (the ruins of which would have been cleared for the building of the church) — the area the Samaritans still venerate.

Left:
The Nablus Area

The Healing God's Shrine at Bethzatha

The general area of Bethzatha is well known. The Byzantine church immediately located it at two large reservoirs north of the city. Josephus called this district "Bethzetha." Ancient manuscripts of the New Testament call it "Bethzatha." Although "Bethesda" (the common English name) also has a good textual tradition, we use "Bethzatha" following the RSV.

The Turks gave the area of these reservoirs to France in 1856, but the reservoirs themselves were not uncovered until 1872. In 1878 they became the property of the White Fathers.

Bethzatha at the north of Jerusalem with the two large reservoirs.

Excavations show that the two pools were formed by building a dam across a valley. A Byzantine church was built on the middle of the dam to which supporting arches were added to give the church more floor space. The church's sanctuary was extended over the area beside the pool. St. Mary's birthplace was marked by the church, as was the healing recorded in John 5.

John 5: 1-18

The pools fell into disuse and gradually filled with debris. In A.D. 614, Persians (pagans who wreaked destruction throughout the Holy Land) leveled the church and hastened the complete filling of the area. The site was neglected during the following Muslim period. Crusaders built a small chapel in the vicinity of the ruins of the Byzantine church. A larger church, dedicated to St. Anne, the mother of Mary, was also built in this area. The site now seems to be as important for the remembrance of St. Mary as for the healing in John. The chapel over the pools fell into ruins after the defeat of the Crusaders in 1187. St. Anne's remained intact because the Muslim general, Saladin, turned it into a school. Today it is again used as a church.

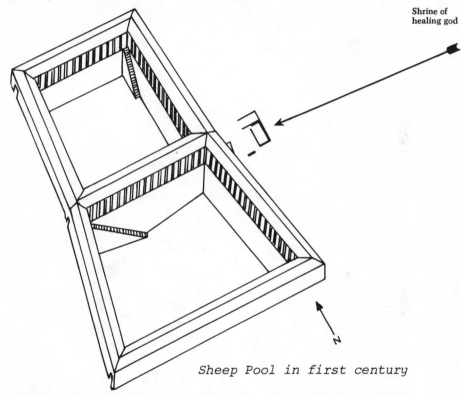

Shrine of healing god

Sheep Pool in first century

The story of the setting of John 5 would have ended at this point had not the White Fathers become interested in the sanctuary area of the Byzantine church. The result of their excavations was both shocking and illuminating. They found a series of grottoes and basins under the sanctuary arranged in a rough circle. Votive objects found in this area indicate that it was a cult center for the healing god called Serapis in the east, or Asclepius in the west. Most of the ruins date from the later Roman period — the period just before the Byzantines covered the shrine with the sanctuary. Careful study of the area has led A. Duprez to conclude that the shrine was present in the first century as well. One wonders if this area was covered by the sanctuary because of Byzantine uneasiness with Jesus' presence in such a place. Verse four of John 5 (correctly omitted by most translations as late) may have been inserted for the same reason.

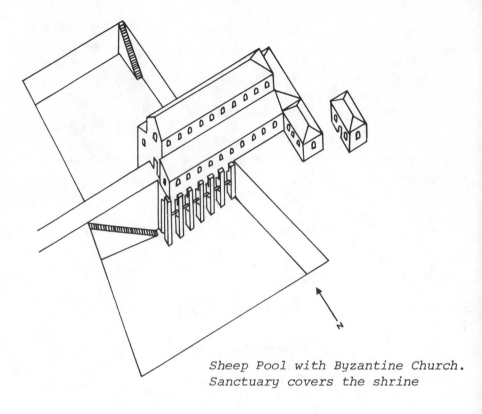

Sheep Pool with Byzantine Church.
Sanctuary covers the shrine

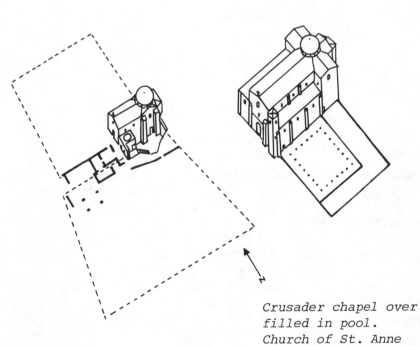

Crusader chapel over
filled in pool.
Church of St. Anne
in area of former shrine

It is now easier to understand the first verse of John 5, which locates the event. The "Sheep Pool" must refer to the large basins, and the subject (which is understood in the sentence but not given) is not a "pool" or a "gate" as sometimes supplied in translations, but rather a "place" called Bethzatha. This must have been the name of the healing center. We translate the opening verse "Now there is in Jerusalem by the Sheep Pool a place, called in Hebrew, Bethzatha, which has five porches."

This removes some of the difficulties in John 5. Now we understand why the cripple is pictured as anything but an example of a firm believer. It was difficult to imagine the encounter taking place at the two reservoirs. If "The Feast" was Succoth (we accept this as the festival because good manuscripts read that Jesus went up to *the* feast — another name for Succoth), the pools would have been about empty. To *throw* someone into them (as the Greek reads in 5:7), would probably result in a broken leg or neck! If the pool was full, there must have been a number of drownings. Now we know the setting is one of the shallow pools in the shrine.

The location of such a place near the Temple (the pagan-dominated Antonia was also in this area) is less surprising the more we picture Jerusalem in Jesus' day with people who are as human as those in our communities. Not all the People of God in Jerusalem were extremely devout. Congregations are never perfect in any time or place. When a terminal illness strikes, some of God's People will try any means to hold onto their life, sacrificing or compromising their faith if they must — just like that 38-year sufferer Jesus meets at Bethzatha.

For further study:

A. Duprez, *Jésus et les Dieux Guérisseurs, Cahiers de la Revue Biblique,* 12 (Paris: Gabalda, 1970). There is a good summary of this work in English by W. D. Davies, *The Gospel and the Land* (Berkeley: Un. of California Press, 1974) 302-313.

Where Were the 5,000 Fed?

The location of the feeding of the 5,000 is one of the factors which has led some scholars to conclude that the order of chapters in John is incorrect. They cannot understand how it is possible to speak of Jesus crossing "to the other side of the Sea of Galilee" (John 6:1) when He is in Jerusalem in 5:47. Of course, the main influence on these scholars is the other Gospels and, more precisely, Luke. He places the Feeding on the east shore of the lake, not far from Bethsaida (Luke 9:10). Accepting this location, many conclude Jesus must be crossing from the west to the east shore in John's account. Because that direction does not fit travel from Jerusalem, they conclude chapter six should come before chapter five. When John's Gospel is allowed to stand on its own, the present order is no longer problematic. It *is* possible to cross the Sea of Galilee from *south to north,* as well as from west to east! The former fits the travel route from Jerusalem.

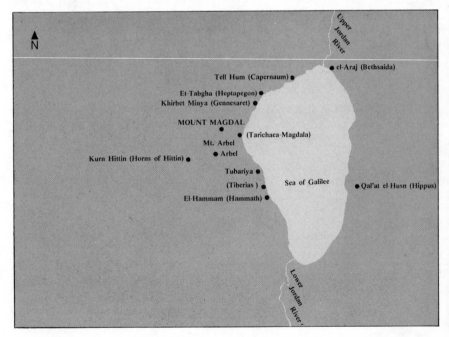

Sea of Galilee

A close look at the variants for the first verse of chapter six is also helpful. The common text used for translation has a rather awkward construction of two genitives reading "the other side of the Sea *of* Galilee *of* Tiberias." However, one of the earliest manuscripts reads: "Jesus went to the other side of the Sea of Galilee *to the region of Tiberias.*" A student of the ancient manuscripts, M. E. Boismard, chooses this as the most plausible reading *(Revue Biblique,* 64 [1957]

369 and *Revue Biblique* 60 [1953] 362). Rather than the usual pattern of later scribes making a difficult reading smoother, we have just the opposite as scribes tried to bring John into better harmony with Luke. The precision found in this early manuscript fits John's concern that the reader picture the setting.

"The region of Tiberias" still does not indicate exactly where the feeding took place on the west shore. Pilgrim accounts from the Byzantine and Crusader periods are not very helpful. The Byzantines decided on a spot that follows neither Luke on the east shore, nor John on the west shore. They compromised and built their church on the north shore at et-Tabgha (this is an Arabized form of Heptapegon, the ancient Greek name of this small plain). This church was excavated in 1932. See A. M. Schneider, *The Church of the Multiplying of the Loaves and Fishes at Tabgha* (London: Caldwell, 1937). Visitors can still admire its excellent mosaics.

Not all pilgrim accounts are in agreement with this location. J. P. MacPherson, in his translation of the pilgrimage account of Arculfus notes, "Tradition at present points to the brow of the hill between Kurn Hattin and Tiberias as the spot." *Pilgrimage of Arculfus* (London: Palestine Pilgrims' Text Society, [1895] 44).

John's Gospel supports this location. John 6:23 states that on the next day people from Tiberias came near the place where the 5,000 were fed. From there they sailed to Capernaum. This harbor was located three or four miles from the shore where the disciples landed when heading for Capernaum (John 6:19). Taricheae fits both incidents. Mount Arbel blocks easy access by land to Tiberias, making the use of small boats more convenient, as we see in John's Gospel. Josephus also traveled by boat between the two cities *(Life,* 156).

In this area there are two good candidates for *the* mount. Mount Arbel, which attracted MacPherson, is the more dramatic of the two. The caves in its high cliffs would serve as a perfect place for retreat. The side of Arbel is, however, steep and difficult to climb.

The other mount is located directly behind Taricheae and centered on the southern part of the Gennesaret Plain. This is known today as Mount Magdal. Its high point is located to the west, leaving a long, lower stoop which overlooks the plain. Although Mount Magdal is lower than Arbel, its central position sets it apart. The lower area is very suitable for addressing a crowd, while the higher ground is far enough removed from the plain to allow retreat from crowds. We have chosen this as *the* mount in our reconstruction.

For a good summary of the history of Tiberias, see
M. Avi-Yonah, "The Foundations of Tiberias," *Israel Exploration Journal,* 1 (1950-51) 160.

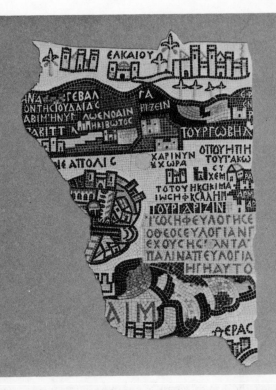

Ephraim

John's Gospel has a very different sequence of events for the last week of Jesus' ministry. Settings differ as well. Matthew, Mark, and Luke describe Jesus' last trip to Jerusalem for the Passover as a journey from the Galilee, which passes through the Jericho area and culminates with a grand entry into the Temple area. John, however, reports that the last autumn of Jesus' ministry is spent in Jerusalem, not the Galilee. The last time He travels the Jericho road is in the middle of winter when He returns from exile in Peraea to raise Lazarus. This event is immediately followed by retreat to Ephraim, which John notes is "near the wilderness" (11:54). Perhaps Ephraim is not well known today because it was a place for retreat, far from public roads which pilgrims of all times seem to favor.

The Byzantine church, to be sure, did not ignore Johannine geography. The Madaba map locates Ephraim east of Bethel, not far from Rimmon in the hills beside the Jordan Valley. Interestingly, there is no indication of a church on the map, but simply the crowded wording "Ephron or Ephraea, the Lord came from there." Eusebius also notes Ephraim's location. He is very precise in his description, asserting that it is 20 miles north of Jerusalem and five miles to the east of Bethel *(Onomasticon* 90,19; 28,4). Jerome follows his indentification. This has led many to suppose that et-Taiybe was formerly Ephraim.

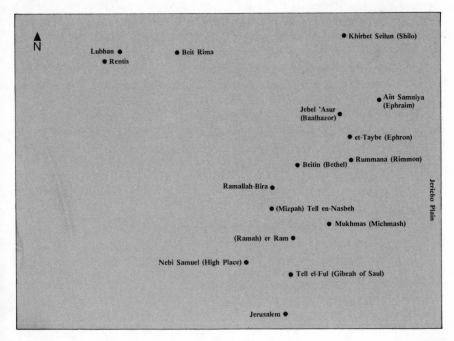

Ain Samniye

Left:
Part of the Madaba map.

This identification has much to recommend it. The name of the village, "Taiybe" means *good* in Arabic. The residents of this Christian Arab village are aware that this is a relatively recent name. Previously their town was called "Afra." Unfortunately, "Afra" has a bad connotation in Arabic, meaning *dirty*. The villagers decided to turn the name of their town into a *good* one! Is "Afra," then, a shortened form of Ephraim?

The ruin of a Byzantine church at et-Taiybe is still an important center for worship. The remembrance, however, is *not* of Jesus' sojourn at Ephraim. It is dedicated to St. George. A. M. Schneider, who surveyed the Byzantine church, feels that it probably always was dedicated to St. George. Perhaps et-Taiybe-Afra is Ophra or Ephron of the ancient world and not Ephraim. Ophra, of the Old Testament would fit et-Taiybe perfectly (1 Samuel 13:17, Joshua 18:23, 2 Chronicles 13:19). In the first century A. D., Josephus mentions an Ephron,*War* IV, 551 but not Ephraim. This must be the same as Ophra.

There is also an "Ephraim" in the Old Testament which is described near Mount Baalhazor, located to the north of et-Taiybe (2 Samuel 13:23). In the Talmud *(b. Menahot* 83b), Ephraim is mentioned as being near Michmash. The location, however, is not, as et-Taiybe's, on a hill, but rather in a valley or a plain that produces wheat. From Baalhazor in the direction of the desert (following John's note), there is only one major valley with an ancient village that produces wheat — Ain Samniya. This is where Albright, followed by Schneider, suggests that Ephraim should be located. In his *Gazeteer of Roman Palestine,* Avi-Yonah (who did extensive work in the location of sites in the period of the New Testament) also supports this location.

Ain Samniya does fit the Madaba map, being closer to the edge of the hills bordering the Jericho Plain than et-Taiybe. The distances given by Eusebius, although roughly fitting et-Taiybe, better fit Ain Samniya. This valley also is a better place for retreat. It would not easily be discovered or readily reported. Witness how few travelers make their way to the valley today! The Lutheran World Federation, only a decade ago, provided the first access road to help the people of the valley move their produce more easily to the markets in the villages above. Potsherds scattered about the valley indicate at a glance that this site has a very rich history, beginning in the Bronze Age.

The valley would provide a good temporary retreat center in winter. It is warm because of its low position, and its spring provides plenty of water. All around the valley are shallow caves where the disciples could make their temporary camp, as Bedouin do today.

For further study:

W. F. Albright, "Ophrah and Ephraim," *Annual of the American Schools of Oriental Research,* 4 (1922-23) 124-133.

A. M. Schneider, "Die Kirche von et-Taiybe," *Oriens Christianus,* 6 (1931) 15-22. For the location of Ephraim at et-Taiybe see C. Kopp, *Holy Places of the Gospels* (New York: Herder, 1963) 254-256.

The Setting of the Crucifixion

Today, the area of the crucifixion is called the Muristan. By reviewing the remains from the first century found in various parts of the Muristan, we can reconstruct how this area appeared on Good Friday.

THE STONE QUARRY: Lutheran Church of the Redeemer, Martin Luther School.

Many have assumed that the wall of Jerusalem in the days of Jesus passed under the Lutheran Church of the Redeemer. This was due to C. Schick's (a German architect employed by the Turks at the end of the last century) claim to have seen it. When Redeemer Church was restored in 1970, U. Lux excavated underneath the church to study this wall. What was uncovered could not have been a city wall from Jesus' day. It was probably a terrace wall from the Byzantine period. It rests on 25 feet of fill! A shaft dug through the fill revealed partly quarried stones and quarrying cuts. Since potsherds in the soil immediately above bedrock are Herodian, it is supposed that Herod the Great used the quarry. The results of this excavation complement those of K. M. Kenyon. In the early sixties, she dug a shaft in the Martin Luther School playground 70 yards south of the Lux dig. At the same depth, Kenyon also found what appeared to be a stone quarry. This picture would have come into focus much earlier had relationships between France and Prussia been better. When Redeemer Church was being built from 1893 to 1898, P. Groth, the architect for the Prussians, refused to allow the French to observe the new foundation shafts. He, of course, had discovered the quarry. At this time, L. H. Vincent, the French Dominican, was gathering material for his monumental work on Jerusalem of the Old and New Testaments, but was never allowed to study this area. Groth's material was never published, having been destroyed in a bombing raid over Germany during the Second World War. Fortunately, Groth's secret accounting report came to light as the Lux dig was getting under way. The figures given in the report help us to reconstruct the depth of the quarry. From the Lux shaft, the quarry floor drops about two yards farther to the north. The excavations carried out in the basement of Alexander Church across the street from Redeemer Church indicate that the quarry wall rose steeply in this area. To the east, the quarry must also have such a wall, as the bedrock is not far below the marketplace of Suq *(Market)* el-Atarrin. The depth of the foundation of the bell tower of Redeemer Church indicates that the quarry floor rises four yards to the west of the Lux shaft. The hill rising to the Lutheran Guest House behind David Street is the extent of the quarry to the south. The fill Kenyon and Lux removed from above bedrock was evidently put there by

Hadrian in the second century when he turned this area into the forum of his pagan Jerusalem, Aelia Capitolina.

For further study:

K. M. Kenyon *Digging Up Jerusalem* (New York: Praeger, 1974) 226-235.

U. Lux, "Vorlaufiger Bericht Über die Ausgrabung unter der Erlöserkirche," *Zeitschrift des deutschen Palästina-Vereins* (1972) 186-199.

GOLGOTHA AND THE TOMB: The Church of the Resurrection*
Eusebius, *Life of Constantine,* III

Excavations in the Church of the Resurrection show that the deep quarry under the Lutheran property probably was entered from this area. In 1974, Ch. Coüasnon, the late Dominican architect for the restoration of the Church of the Resurrection, had the opportunity to lay a small trench to the south of the Christ's tomb. About a yard and a half below the floor surface he, too, uncovered a quarry similar to that under Redeemer Church. The first level of the quarry evidently was cut into the hillside to the west of the Resurrection Church on which the thickly-populated Christian Quarter now rests. The limestone formation in this part of the hill was evidently of such poor quality that part of the hill was left standing as rock was quarried around it. It must have given the impression of a skull; hence it was called Golgotha.

In the first century, wealthy persons purchased abandoned quarries for their family tombs, as did Joseph of Arimathea. The wall left in the hill by the quarry was perfect for the beginning of a tomb. The quarried section between Golgotha and the tomb was later filled in again by Hadrian to create an acropolis for his forum. This inadvertently preserved both Golgotha and the tomb. When Constantine came into power, he was urged to pull down the temple to Aphrodite or Zeus on the acropolis and clear away the debris beneath. The tomb and Golgotha emerged from almost two centuries of burial! Later the tomb chamber in which Jesus had been laid was freed from the hill behind. Over this chamber, a huge dome was constructed. Golgotha was enclosed in a porch, and a huge cathedral was built facing the tomb. This church was badly damaged in 614 by the pagan Persians. In 1009, all but a remnant of the tomb was hacked away by the fanatic Walid. The Crusaders built the present church which covers the tomb and Golgotha.

For further study:

Ch. Coüasnon, *The Church of the Holy Sepulchre in Jerusalem* (London: Oxford Un. Press, 1974).

J. Jeremias, *Heiligen Gräber in Jesus Umwelt* (Göttingen: Ruprecht, 1958). Part III is helpful for understanding the importance of tombs in the first century.

---

*Westerners usually refer to this as the "Church of the Holy Sepulchre." This is unfortunate. The Eastern Church's designation, "Church of the Resurrection," certainly captures more accurately the meaning of this place.

J. Wilkinson, *Egeria's Travels* (London: SPCK, 1971) gives a Byzantine pilgrim's view of the church.

THE SECOND WALL: Suq el-Atarrin
Josephus, *War,* V, 147.

The battle among scholars over the lines of the walls of the first century Jerusalem has been fierce. This is particularly true of the "second wall" — the name Josephus gives the most recent wall in Jesus' day. One reason for the battle is the Church of the Resurrection. Was its property inside or outside the wall in Jesus' day? The great fuss is over a very short wall. Josephus describes it in a sentence:

> The second wall started from the gate in the first wall which they called Gennath *(Garden Gate)* enclosing only the northern district of the town; it circled up to the Antonia. *(War,* V, 146)

Vincent, following the supposed part of the wall under Redeemer Church, proposed a line whose course insured Golgotha was outside the city. His wall met the "first wall" by the citadel area. Following the discovery of the quarry, it became apparent that Vincent's line for the wall and most Bible atlases and models of the first century Jerusalem are incorrect.

The quarry under the Lutheran property would be an excellent defense moat for the "second wall." This means that the "second wall" should be sought behind the quarry along the line Dalman suggested early in this century. He has been followed by Kenyon, Lux, Benoit, and Avi-Yonah. Evidently this quarry-moat forced the Romans to bring their battering ram against the northern side of the second wall, not the west side as would have been expected before the quarry was discovered *(War,* V, 317).

Since the second wall is described as "circling up to the Antonia," it must turn at the corner of the quarry, cross over and enclose the flat Ros Golgotha, and then descend to the Tyropoeon Valley, on the other side of which it joined the Antonia.

For further study:

L. H. Vincent, *Jérusalem de L'Ancien Testament* (Paris: Gabalda, 1954) 90-113.

J. Simon, "The 'Second Wall' and the Problem of the Holy Sepulchre," *Jerusalem in the Old Testament* (Leiden: Brill, 1952) 282-343.

M. Avi-Yonah "The Third and Second Walls of Jerusalem," *Israel Exploration Journal,* 18 (1968) 98-125.

THE FIRST WALL: Lutheran Guest House, "David's Tower".
Josephus, *War,* V, 142-145.

The "second wall" was probably built by Herod the Great. If older, we would expect Josephus to note this by ascribing it to Solomon, as he does the

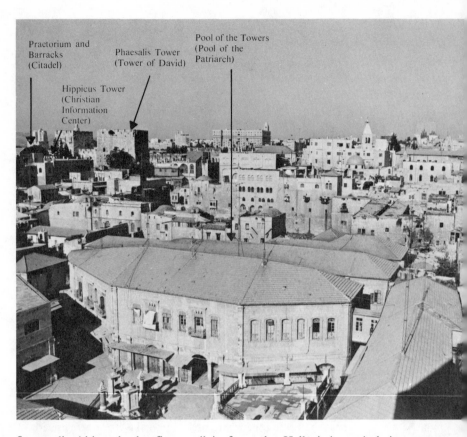

Praetorium and
Barracks
(Citadel)

Hippicus Tower
(Christian
Information
Center)

Phaesalis Tower
(Tower of David)

Pool of the Towers
(Pool of the
Patriarch)

first wall. Although the first wall is from the Hellenistic period, its stones, recognized as being pre-Herodian in style, led Josephus to label the wall Solomonic. The "Porch of Solomon" (John 10:23) referring to the Hellenistic part of the Temple area is another example of this. The line of the first wall runs along the hillside above David Street. Just east of the Lutheran Guest House (through which the first wall once passed) this hill drops off, depriving the wall of its natural protection. Evidently the "Garden Gate" was near here. The second wall, itself well protected by the quarry, served to secure the weak eastern part of the first wall.

Herod the Great strengthened the first wall and built three towers into its weakest point, the present Jaffa Gate area. The magnificent Tower of Hippicus probably rose where the Christian Information Center now stands. The so-called "Tower of David" across the street from the Center is the Phaesalis Tower. A third and smaller tower Mariamme, was added to the wall to the west of Phaesalis.

THE POOL OF THE TOWERS: Pool of the Patriarch
Josephus, *War*, V, 468.

Just outside Hippicus Tower was a large reservoir. A shallow valley descending to the east begins in the area of this reservoir, becoming much deeper

Golgotha
(Church of
Resurrection)

Tomb

The Muristan
from Redeemer
Church Tower

after passing through the stone quarry. The valley was deepened and dammed to make the reservoir. Today it is the filled-in Pool of the Patriarch behind Christian Quarter Road. Its water was brought through a small gate beside Hippicus Tower *(War,* V, 284, 305).

THE PALACE OF HEROD THE GREAT AND THE BARRACKS: The Citadel and Armenian School

Josephus, *War,* I, 402; II, 329; V, 176-182.

Just inside the towers and running south along the high ridge was the palace of Herod the Great. Behind the towers was a barracks area today called "The Citadel." The outer wall of the Citadel by Jaffa Gate was built by the Crusaders, leaving the foundations of the city wall and barracks in Jesus' day inside the Citadel. These have been carefully excavated by C. N. Johns and R. Amiran. Their findings show that Herod built his palace on a platform, leaving the walls of earlier houses underneath for further support. More of the platform was uncovered before the Armenians built their new school. It is evidently this platform which gave the name "Gabatha," *Elevated Place,* to the pavement between the two buildings of the palace complex (John 19:13). All of the structures above the platform were destroyed by the Romans *(War,* V, 182-183;

II, 431-440). We must rely on Josephus for the only decription of what was the most magnificent building in Jerusalem.

For further study:

C. N. Johns, "The Citadel, Jerusalem — A Summary of Work Since 1934," *Quarterly of the Department of Antiquities in Palestine,* 5 (1936) 121.

R. Amiran, "Excavations in the Jerusalem Citadel," *Jerusalem Revealed.*

THE PRAETORIUM: The Armenian School
Josephus, *War,* II, 301-308, 328-329.

That the Praetorium was located at the Antonia north of the Temple area has been a basic assumption for several centuries. This, however, has been seriously questioned in this century. Dalman showed that it was not this barracks in which the procurator resided, but rather the palace of Herod. This was later supported by Benoit's careful study. His conclusions are today generally accepted by students of the setting of New Testament Jerusalem. Like the later procurators, Pilate resided in the fine palace which had once served Herod the Great. It was located in the cooler, cleaner, and well protected Upper City.

For further study:

P. Benoit, "Pretoire, Lithostroton et Gabbatha," *Revue Biblique,* 59 (1952) 531-550.

G. Dalman, *Sacred Sites and Ways,* 335-347.

For the arguments for the Antonia as Praetorium, see M. Aline de Sion, *La Forteresse Antonia à Jérusalem et la Question de Prétoire* (Jerusalem: Franciscan Press, 1955). The Game of the King is discussed in this work (119-142). An example of this is found on the second century pavement below the Sisters of Zion.

THE VIA DOLOROSA: Citadel, David Street, Christian Quarter Road

This location of the Praetorium changes the Via Dolorosa from that traditionally followed. Dalman indicated in 1924, and Benoit in 1952, that the way actually was from the Citadel to the Church of the Resurrection. The location of the place "outside" the Praetorium where the way begins is not certain. Dalman understands John to mean the entire compound of the Herodian Palace and suggests that the judgment seat was placed at one of its entrances. For the purposes of our reconstruction, we have chosen instead to locate the part of the compound not entered by the People as the palace building itself. The grounds outside the palace would not be an area where priests would worry anymore about uncleanness, as any other open area of the city.

The route to Golgotha is not difficult to reconstruct. Passing out of the city through the small gate by the Hippicus Tower, the reservoir would force the way to descend between it and the hillside supporting the first wall. This is the present David Street. From the corner of the pool, the way would gently descend to the place of the crucifixion near Christian Quarter Road. Much of the original Way of the Cross is probably now covered by shops.

*Joseph's Hometown**

Arimathea, also Samuel's hometown (Ramathaim-zophim — 1 Samuel 1:1) is located in a bewildering diversity of places.

Nebi Samuel, the traditional site, has been eliminated as a candidate because of the identification of el-Jib below it as Gibeon. Nebi Samuel was actually Gibeon's high place (2 Samuel 21:9).

Er-Ram, located on the main highway leading to Jerusalem from the north and not far from Tel el-Ful (Gibeah of Saul), preserves the ancient name "Ramah." This must be the Ramah of Judges 19:13 and 1 Kings 15:17, which is not necessarily the same as Samuel's hometown. Ramah, *Height,* is a very common name. The Madaba map has both Ramah and Arimathea. Ramah corresponds to er-Ram. This Ramah does not easily fit the circuit of Samuel (1 Samuel 9:6). Er-Ram also lacks two high places which is what "Ramathaim" indicates, although Mazar *(Israel Exploration Journal,* 4 [1954] 230) contends that the "aim" ending is locative, not dual. The story of the meeting of Saul and Samuel, however, would seem to demand two high places (1 Samuel 9:11-12). Most questionable is the location of er-Ram (as Nebi Samuel) in the tribe of Benjamin and not in Ephraim as 1 Samuel 1:1 demands.

Ramallah, suggested by Albright, has never proved to have an extensive settlement from the period of Samuel.

Rentis, long a favorite of the German School of Archaeology in Jerualem *(Palestina Jahr Buch* [1925] 72), does fit Eusebius' description of Arimathea in the *Onomasticon.* He locates it in terms of Lod which is on the coastal plain. However, Rentis is not in the "hill country" of Ephraim as 1 Samuel 1:1 notes. It is on the edge of the coastal plain.

Beit Rima also fits Eusebius' description, has two high places, and is located in the hill country of Ephraim. O. E. Buhl first suggested this site in 1896. He is followed by E. Schürer in 1901. The arguments for Beit Rima are summarized well by A. M. Wiener, *Journal of the Palestine Oriental Society* (1927) 109.

The amount of space needed to describe the tribe of Benjamin on the Madaba map has forced the artist to shift some of the villages in the tribe of Benjamin. Since the artist did not use the space near the coastal plain for Arimathea, although there is plenty of space, Rentis is further brought into question. The designer of the map thinks of Arimathea as being to the west of Ramah and half-way into the hill country of Ephraim. This fits Beit Rima.

*See map p. 213

Index of Place Names